A child psychiatrist and father of four, Dr. Fass combines both clinical and personal experience to help all parents understand more about their children.

Happily aware of each child's unique quality, Dr. Fass is no alarmist about the "abnormal." He is more concerned with the "do's" than the "dont's" of child rearing.

How to Raise an Emotionally H... ...x-pert's honest, gentle portray... ...and unusual—manifestat... ...wth, beginning at age fifte... ...ng with adolescence.

How to Raise an Emotionally Healthy Child
was originally published by Trident Press,
under the title: *A Primer for Parents*.

HOW TO
RAISE AN
Emotionally
Healthy Child

(Original Title:
A Primer for Parents)

BY

JEROME S. FASS, M.D.

PUBLISHED BY POCKET BOOKS NEW YORK

How to Raise an Emotionally Healthy Child

(Original Title: *A Primer for Parents*)

Trident Press edition published March, 1968

A *Pocket Book* edition
1st printing .... September, 1969

This *Pocket Book* edition includes every word
contained in the original, higher-priced edition. It is printed
from brand-new plates made from completely reset, clear, easy-to-read
type. *Pocket Book* editions are published by Pocket Books, a division
of Simon & Schuster, Inc., 630 Fifth Avenue, New York, N.Y. 10020.
Trademarks registered in the United States and other countries.

Standard Book Number: 671—75395—9.
Library of Congress Catalog Card Number: 68—18317.
Copyright, ©, 1968, by Jerome S. Fass. All rights reserved.

Printed in the U.S.A.

To my wife Joyce—who has made it possible

To my children, Barry, Daniel, Sharon, and Amy—who have made it necessary

Contents

Contents

Contents

Contents

Contents

Contents

Contents

Introduction

Nothing is more difficult, more frustrating, or more conflict-ing—and yet more satisfying and more fulfilling—than having and raising children. I say this from my experience as a child psychiatrist and as the father of two sons and two daughters.

As parents, we are the first stepping stones upon which our children will stand. With our love and guidance our children can take further steps, reach out for other stepping stones—friends, teachers—and ultimately establish a healthy relation-ship with a marriage partner. As parents we have our needs too. Some we can see and feel very readily, and others are not that clearly seen or understood—they are unconscious. It is these unconscious needs that we are going to discuss more fully in this book. Let us see what happens when a need of ours comes into conflict with the needs of our children. What can we do to make things happier for us and healthier for our children?

We parents are forever walking a tightrope, trying to find the correct balance. We ask, for example, when do proper controls become unwarranted restrictions? When is it motiva-tion and when is it pressure? When is it security and when is it overprotection?

It is impossible for us to do the "correct" thing at all times for our children. We're only human and we live with many pressures, whether as a mother having to care for an entire family or as a father trying to earn a living. At times we are going to get rattled and angry. At such times don't begin criticizing yourself as being a poor parent. Where there is love and acceptance, the child is quite capable of tolerating an emotional response of anger from his parents.

Billions of Snowflakes

We have learned a great deal in recent years about how each child differs and how each child's behavior changes with its growth. As a result of this newly discovered knowledge, we are in a much better position today to know what is normal and what is abnormal for a particular child at a particular age. I cannot overemphasize the words "particular child at a particular age." Each child is unique and different from all others. Just as one snowflake appears the same as the next and on very close observation is quite different, so every child on closer observation differs from the next. Each period of months in our development, mentally and physically, also differs from all others.

You may at this point rightfully ask, "If all children are so different, what can I learn from this book that applies to my child?" The answer is that we have to understand these differences and how they develop, how they often change with the months, and what we can and must not do as parents if the very normal process of growing up is to be in a healthy direction.

In understanding our children it will help to know something about the differences we find existing from the moment they are born. If we were to go into a newborn nursery and were to observe the infants crying, eating, sleeping and moving, we could readily hear, see, and even smell the differences among them. One will be crying loudly and harshly, another quite softly. One infant's lips will grap at the nipple or bottle, another will have to be cajoled into taking its nourishment. Some will sleep longer than others and some will sleep more deeply. Careful observations will show that each infant's movements are quite different. Even their urine ar

1

feces will have different odors. Today interesting studies are being made in many institutions by child psychiatrists who are attempting to make long-term personality predictions based upon careful observations of these differences among infants.

It is these very differences that will play a large part in what your child will be like. They will help determine the relationship that will be established between you and your child and consequently between your child and the rest of the world.

No Returns, No Exchanges

When a child is born, the sale is final—no returns, no exchanges. Nor can we reject some part of the child and expect to have a whole, healthy child. We must accept each of our children for what he is—completely. Total acceptance means that we accept the child's sex, his intellectual capabilities, his physical characteristics, his social responsiveness, and his limitations.

Long before our child is born, we have ideas as to what we should like him to be. Many of our desires are based upon how we see ourselves. Our likes and dislikes are often quite apparent. One parent wants a boy, another a girl. Looks, intelligence, social capabilities may mean much to us. But what happens when a perfectly normal child is born and doesn't fit the template designed by a parent? Let us see what happens. Let us see how the unconscious part of our mind plays a dominant role in the shaping of our children's lives.

Only the "A" Was Added

Roberta G. was twenty years old and a senior at college when she first consulted me. Tall and quite pretty, with long blonde hair, she could have been a model. But pretty, feminine clothes were not to her liking. She much preferred the boots and riding breeches she wore the first time I saw her. Galloping a horse alongside her father and younger brother, she presented a picture of radiant health. Yet she was quite ill, and anxious about her relationships with her male and female friends.

As her story developed, one could see the father, visibly disappointed on learning that his first-born was a girl. How

3

was he going to teach her to be a champion rider, as he was? For years Roberta was reminded that the name Robert had already been chosen, as though father's wish would, without a doubt, turn into fact. So the "a" was added—but not much more.

Wherever the child turned, she was reminded that she lacked something, something which her younger brother had. How she tried to be the boy her father still preferred! In her relationship with young men, whether to be a boy or girl became a tremendous conflict. It has taken years of therapy for Roberta to accept the "a" in her name, to accept herself as a woman, though she knows full well that a woman can never be happy if she unconsciously wishes to be a man.

Even Without Silks and Velvets

What of a boy whose mother longs for a girl? E. S. was such a boy. The youngest of four sons, he was seen in consultation at the age of seven. He had a history of difficulty in being separated from his mother, had refused to go to camp, and rarely competed in physical activities with other children. His morbid fear of getting hurt led him to play with younger boys in a protective role. Mrs. S. was a bright, pleasant woman in her late thirties who could not understand her son's behavior. She readily told of wanting a girl after having had three sons. What she could not see clearly at first was that her son quite unconsciously became aware of her desire for a girl and did his utmost to please her. Had she dressed him in silks and velvets it would have been more apparent to others, but often our unspoken feelings have a much greater impact in the shaping of our children than what we actually say.

A Neat Trick

As parents, we have strong feelings about our child's intelligence. We associate intelligence with success and we want our children to be successful. So we motivate them to develop intellectually, and that is fine. But when does healthy motivation become unbearable pressure that stifles any creative ability?

It was not healthy motivation that eight-year-old Charles L. received in his home. His mother requested a consultation because she felt her child was not doing well at school. I tried to schedule an appointment for her. I say "tried" because when I offered her an hour she said she could not come at that time. What about another hour? Still no good. There was an appointment for the younger daughter at the allergist, there was the car pool, there was the hairdresser, there was a meeting of her charity committee. All legitimate reasons for still another appointment time. Within ten minutes of jockeying for an hour it became apparent that the mother was trying to dominate the situation from the outset—and doing it quite unconsciously.

Could I, at this point, tell this to the mother? No. Or we would have a mother banging down the telephone and saying, "That psychiatrist is crazy." So another couple of minutes were spent in getting Mrs. L. to agree to exchange car pool dates, and an appointment hour was finally arrived at.

Mrs. L. appeared precisely at the hour. She was a comely, well-groomed, bright, and articulate woman in her mid-thirties. She came right to the point. Her son, Charles, was not doing well in the third grade. Were there any other difficulties? "Well, yes. He's become aloof towards me. He avoids me."

"What about friends?" I asked her.

"No problems."

"How does he get along with his father?"

"Just fine."

Further questioning did not produce a picture of a disturbed youngster. But what was wrong? A doctor is not consulted unless something hurts.

We began talking about other difficulties existing at home. It became apparent Mrs. L. was not a happy woman. She readily spoke of her disappointment in her husband. Mr. L. was an advertising executive who had recently been passed over for a vice-presidency. It seemed that Mr. L. worked closely with an older friend who had brought him into the agency. Mrs. L. was quite annoyed that her husband shared his ideas freely with him, letting the friend get the credit and eventually the vice-presidency. Most of the session with Mrs. L. was devoted not to talking about her son but rather to harsh criticism of her husband.

My next job was to interview the father and to see school records on Charles.

The difference between Mr. and Mrs. L. was apparent even in the matter of an appointment hour—Mr. L. readily agreed to any hour I had free.

Mr. L. was a tall, heavy-set man of forty with a heavy thatch of unruly black hair. In his rumpled brown suit and stained tie he was not the Hollywood image of a Madison Avenue advertising executive. He spoke slowly in carefully chosen words about what he thought was wrong. He felt that his wife was haranguing him and his son. "I earn a good living, but she always wants more. Charles got an eighty-six in a spelling test, but it wasn't good enough. Doctor, I sincerely believe that it's she who needs the help more than Charles."

During our talk I noticed that Mr. L. reached into his pocket to throw a tablet into his mouth. It was an antacid pill for his newly discovered ulcer.

From the school I learned a great deal more. It seemed that Mrs. L. had approached the teacher and made known her disappointment with Charles's work. The teacher was surprised to hear this and told Mrs. L. that his work was good and that she was satisfied with it. Mrs. L. then began to argue that a boy with an I.Q. of 141 ought to be doing much better. 141? The teacher conferred with the school psychologist, who had an I.Q. of 112 recorded for Charles. A check by him with Mrs. L. revealed that she was referring to a private test she had had Charles take for entrance into a school for exceptionally bright children. The psychologist then agreed that a psychiatric consultation was in order, convinced that such a change within two years was indicative of a severe pathology.

All this was revealed by the school psychologist, whom I knew. What made him so sure that the mother was told that Charles had an I.Q. of 141? "Nothing, but why should I doubt her?"

There was good reason to doubt the mother. A check with the psychologist at the private school revealed that two and a half years before, the mother had had Charles tested and he scored 114. Mother, for her own reasons, simply reversed the last two digits. A neat trick!

A second session left me convinced that Charles did not need help, but that his mother surely did. Sadly, as in many situations in child psychiatry, the family member in need of help spurns it, insisting that there is something wrong with the mate or child. It is then that the child ultimately does need professional help.

Masturbation Is Not Prostitution

Rejection of some part of the child can be the result of unconsciously comparing something about him with something we reject in ourselves or our mate.

I recall the time I was consulted by a distraught mother regarding her five-year-old daughter. The mother was a stocky European woman who had been orphaned during World War II. She had suffered greatly during the war, and out of desperation had turned to prostitution, although still a child of fourteen. She later married and led an exemplary life, and without difficulty raised two fine sons, then aged thirteen and eight.

Now she was having marked difficulties with her five-year-old daughter. She felt her daughter was disrespectful, was too demanding, and complained bitterly about the child's bed-wetting and touching of her genitals. When I saw the mother a second time, she spoke of herself and the great shame she felt for having been a prostitute at such an early age. That was it! She had made an association with what was troubling her so much.

It gave me the opportunity to say, "It seems you're afraid your daughter will be a prostitute as you were."

For a moment she stared straight at me, eyes wide open, not a word said. Slowly she said, "I never thought of that." She was silent for several moments and then said, "I think you're right."

With that, she began to talk more freely of what she felt were her contributions to her difficulty with her daughter. She spoke of how uncomfortable she felt when she saw her daughter coveting her father's attention and how she literally took her off his lap and admonished her to let him eat his meal in peace.

With her unconscious fear more apparent, it did not take long for the mother to accept that for children to handle their genitals is quite normal, and that girls of five do pay attention to and want attention from their fathers. Most important, she came to realize that the lives of the mother and the daughter were quite different and for her child to show some indication of sexual feeling did not mean that she was heading towards a life of promiscuity or prostitution.

A Nose Is a Nose Is a Nose

Here I should like to tell you of the numerous times I have seen children and adults react, consciously and unconsciously, to the rejection of some physical characteristic by one or both parents.

I may, by now, sound critical of parents. I do not mean to do so. I only ask that we be able to accept our children's physical characteristics as they are, that we not undermine their self-images by pointing out to others or to them what we see and don't like. It is true that other children will very likely pick on some not-so-pretty physical characteristic. But as parents we do have enormous power to deter and negate destructive self-feelings when they occur. We want our children to succeed in life. Let us help them develop an image of themselves that will give them confidence. As a song of the early 1940's puts it—"Let us accentuate the positive—eliminate the negative."

Let us stop comparing our children to some hypothetical norm or to other children. Each child is unique. Some will grow tall and others short. Some will be thin and some heavy. Some will have long noses and others will have short noses. Some will have large ears and some will have little ears. Some will be dark-complexioned and others light-complexioned. Some will develop acne and others will not. It should not matter. Of greatest importance is the emotional health of the individual.

In all areas, whether it be school or athletics or physical

beauty, our children will do enough self-examination and comparing. Their friends will certainly add their critical comments. As parents we must show our acceptance in full if they are to develop a healthy image of themselves.

Failure at Seven, Hero at Eleven

A Kaleidoscope

Children's emotions as they grow remind me of a kaleidoscope. Just as we look into the kaleidoscope to see the many changing colors and geometric forms, so with our children we can see the many changes taking place before our eyes.

As I write this, I am smiling as I recall an incident which occurred only yesterday. Our son, Barry, came home two days ago all excited about the fourth-grade music program at school. He was to be taught to play an instrument, and he had decided to study the violin. Fine. I made plans to stop off at the music shop and discuss renting an instrument. Experience had shown me that buying it might be wasteful, knowing how the kaleidoscope of a child's mind changes. Even so, I was not quite prepared for his request yesterday. It went as follows: "Dad, could we go down to Clayton's and pick up a trombone?"

"A trombone? I thought you wanted a violin."

"But Dad, that was yesterday."

My wife and I looked at each other and began to laugh. Barry, at that point, walked out the door munching on a MacIntosh and looking at us with an expression that seemed to say, "What's so funny about a kid changing his mind?" Two hours later it was the violin again. It seemed that on his trip outdoors he learned that, "as a violin player you get more chances to play at school."

Just as a child's feelings about a toy or instrument shift, so they also change regarding his school work; his image of himself; his relationship to his peers, to his siblings, and to you.

No Crystal Ball

How often parents think, "Why was I so worried?" There would be less worrying if we knew from the outset how the developing child does change, not only physically but emotionally as well. Too often we see a child having difficulties in a certain area and we begin to make dire predictions about his future. But we don't have a crystal ball and our pessimism is often proven wrong weeks, months, or perhaps years later. Many of us are familiar with famous people such as Einstein, who had difficulty in his early years of schooling, and Winston Churchill, who was considered a failure in his early years by his father. For every famous person considered a failure in his early years there are millions of children who were also so considered and who have succeeded quite handsomely in later years.

Too often a child, instead of being seen as a distinct individual with his own rate of development, is compared to other children or to some hypothetical norm.

Fortunately for Eric D., his parents could appreciate and accept him as an individual. When it came to sports or activity requiring fine coordination, he was a complete failure. It was trying for Eric and his parents when he was seven and was never chosen to play in a baseball game or in other sports. But Eric was interested in biology and science and devoured any book on these subjects. With the support of his parents, Eric could better ward off the rejection of his peers for his clumsiness on the baseball diamond. He more than made up for it by excelling in sciences at school. By the time he was eleven, the heroes of the baseball diamond were flocking to his house to ask for his help with school reports and in the construction of science projects.

Clear Skies and Stormy Days

Although each child differs from the next, observation of large numbers of children reveals that we can usually know in advance when storm clouds approach. With some there seem always to be clear skies and smooth sailing. With others, it seems as though it's a never-ending storm. Is one mentally healthier than the other? Not necessarily so. Let us remember that the sailboat, even in clear weather, always dips and pitches; so it is with children as they grow emotionally. Often parents become concerned about some form of behavior they find disturbing. "What am I doing wrong?" they ask. Very often the answer is "Nothing."

Children have their difficult days, weeks, and sometimes, months. And easy days, weeks and months. Sometimes some event in their lives, such as the birth of a sibling, has a determining effect on their behavior. But more often the changes we see are changes within the child, or are the child's way of growing emotionally as he contends with pressures from within and from without. At times, the child seems at war with himself and the world; at times he is at peace with himself and others.

I should like to describe what we may find at various ages. Again, each child is unique. These are common but by no means universal findings:

I am going to begin at fifteen months because in a number of children I have seen the onset of their difficulties traced to that age. It is then that a sense of independence develops in the child as it is able to move about more freely. If the infant with its nightly demands of feeding and diaper changing seemed difficult, this age is even more tiring for the mother. The child has boundless energy and some mothers are so overwhelmed with caring for the toddler that a difficult relationship begins to be established between mother and child.

Please Listen and Understand Me

If the child were able to express himself this is what we might hear:

I am fifteen months old, so let me go.

I am fifteen months old and love to move about. It's a big, wide, wonderful world filled with drawers and cabinets that I want to look into and try to pull things out of. I have lots of energy, more than Mommy. I hate the playpen and if she puts me into it I'll scream till I'm blue in the face. The only thing it's good for is throwing things into.

I want to be independent, I like it. I know Mommy seems angry when I spill things on the floor, but how else can I learn? I can't hold the spoon or cup too good but I want to try and eat by myself just like Mommy and Daddy. It's lots of fun and I'll smile when I succeed, but please don't frown so much when I fail and you have to clean it up.

Sometimes Mommy ought to get someone to help her with me because surely she needs a rest, trying to keep up with me. It has to be someone I can love and trust so when she is not there I won't feel frightened and lonely.

I can't talk like Mommy and Daddy, but I'll point and try to tell you what I want.

I am eighteen months old. I will do as I please and when I please—now!

I run a little better than three months ago and feel even more independent. I can even climb up stairs but I'm still clumsy and fall and get hurt. When Mommy calls me I like to run the other way. I'll only go to her when I want something. Just because I have so much energy and run so much and make so many demands, I wish Mommy wouldn't think of me as a monster. I can't talk well enough to say what I want or feel, so I get frustrated and have tantrums. I'm not bad, I'm only a normal eighteen-month-old baby trying to grow up.

I am two years old. We can both relax.

I am much better coordinated and organized than I was six months ago. I'm not as frustrated because I can talk now and tell you what I need and want.

Now I walk instead of toddle and Mommy is more relaxed. She doesn't have to worry about my falling so much or about my using a spoon and cup. I spill much less. Mommy seems delighted and I try to please her, but Mommy and Daddy have to realize that I won't be a pleasant two-year-old for very long—I will have to go through more periods of stresses and strains. I need their love, acceptance, and understanding as I try to grow up.

I am two and a half years old. The answer is NO.

I have a strong need to be in complete control. I don't like changes in routine and someone has to help me make decisions. Sometimes I can't decide what to do or wear. These months are very difficult for me and you will have to understand. But soon I will feel under less pressure and so will you.

I am three and a delightful me.

Now I can talk more and better. I am not so frightened of changes in routine and instead of always saying NO, I like to say YES. I will even play and share my toys with others.

I'm three and a half, it's war again.

I've just had a period of calm and now I am passing through a period of stress. Sometimes I show the physical signs of emotional stress. At times I may even stutter, be clumsy, or have a tic, maybe suck my thumb or masturbate. At times I'm going to whine and be demanding.

I'm four and "You make do-do on the floor."

I'm four and love to use dirty words, especially involving the toilet. I feel I can do almost anything. I feel exuberant, even though I don't know what the word means. I have a real good imagination and sometimes I don't know where my fantasy ends and the real world begins. I love to feel independent and if you try to walk with me I'll run ahead of you.

I'm four and a half. I can play better.

I'm not as bouncy as six months ago. I can play better with other boys and girls, so I'm ready to be in groups with them. I'm better able to know what is real and what is imagined.

I'm five. I feel able and stable.

I am much more content with myself and the world. I won't find it hard to do the things you ask of me. It is a less difficult time for me and I seem more able to adjust to stresses such as going off to school.

I'm six and flying again.

I'm flying in all directions and trying new things, but I'm not really sure of myself. At times I'll succeed and laugh, and at other times I'll fail and cry and have a tantrum. But Mom, please be patient with me. I'm trying to grow up, and it isn't easy.

I'm seven and sometimes I want to be alone.

At times I may appear depressed and even paranoid. Sometimes I feel the world is against me. Sometimes I think I was adopted. One day my teacher will be kinder to me, and another day I think she is against me—and the same is true of my friends and brothers and sisters. My younger sister thinks I'm a pest and Mommy wishes I would grow out of this stage a little faster.

I'm eight, so I'll open the gate.

I think I'm going to leave the shell I had at seven. I feel as though I'm ready for a more adult relationship with my friends and family. It is easier for me to give and take—at times I'm more thoughtful and sensitive and more interested in what is happening to my friends and family. But when I'm hurt I'm going to get back into my shell again, and at times I'm going to need a lot of reassurance.

I'm nine, I think I'll try the wine.

I'm nine and I'm much more sure of myself. I'm beginning to feel like a young adult and I don't need your counseling any more. My friends are all I need, but actually I may become very nervous when I think of all the things I have to do at school and how sometimes my friends are better than I am at certain things like playing baseball. I need to feel that I am just as good as they are. I may seem brave, but really I'm very scared at times.

I'm ten years old, and aren't I nice?

Somehow I find it easier to live with myself and with my parents. I seem to be at peace with the world again. Isn't it nice that I can say YES again? I may even be willing to go with you on a trip—I wouldn't even have thought of doing that a year ago.

Whining and Dining

That romantic period when a couple wine and dine by candlelight is often responsible for a period of whining and dining for three or more. The grasping of food by the mouth is instinctual, but parents face eating problems that are often not simple.

The Beginning of a Relationship

From the beginning eating is the center of the first relationship between the child and his mother. To the infant, being held and fed means much, and holding the infant has much emotional meaning to the mother. It is when both mother and child can feel, "This is mine. We belong to each other." Encased in his mother's arms the infant is fed and given a feeling of warmth and security as well. And mother feels gratified and contented. It is a time when the mother should be comfortably at ease so that a sense of warmth, comfort, and security is imparted to the child. This need for the mother's comfort and ease raises a question which "experts" have discussed for decades, since the invention of babies' bottles and infants' formulas.

"Only Breast-Fed Need Apply"

"Should I breast-feed?" is a question often raised by mothers. The answer is quite simple. What will make you feel most comfortable? You want to breast-feed and are willing to accept the inconveniences? Fine! You dislike the idea and want to bottle-feed the infant? That's fine too. As long as you are comfortable in what you are doing. That is the important issue. Warmth, love, and tenderness is imparted by the whole mother, not just a part of her. Today's modern formulas will nourish a child physically as well as a breast and, in some instances, better.

There are "experts" who will tell you that breast-feeding is very important for the emotional stability of the infant and there are "experts" who will tell you that breast-feeding can lead to cancer of the breast. Nonsense! There is no validity to either of these arguments. If breast-feeding was so important to the emotional well-being of the child, and, later, of the adult, then we would expect to read in help-wanted columns such headings as, "Only Breast-Fed Need Apply."

As a psychiatrist in the U.S. Navy, one of my duties was to screen candidates for nuclear submarine duty. We were seeking men who would have stability under stressful conditions. If there was any positive correlation between emotional stability in the adult and breast-feeding, I'm certain we would have questioned each and every candidate about whether he was breast-fed or not—at the expense of some incredulous stares.

Time Clocks Are for Factories

When we consider how each child's needs are different, we can see the fallacy in feeding a child on a rigid schedule with a precise quantity of food at a precise hour. It would be like trying to drive a twelve-cylinder Packard and a Volkswagen the same distance, using the same quantity of gasoline. Sounds silly, doesn't it? Yet this is what some mothers do with food. Just as gasoline is a fuel which drives the car engine, so food is a fuel which gives us the energy to drive our muscles. Each of us has a specific "built-in engine" and "built-in clock" which regulates how much food we need and when we need it. Picture millions of different model cars with different engines and you get the picture of how much one of us differs from the next in his need for food. Those infants who always seem to be eating and those who never seem to want to eat can present a problem to the worried parent. Here your doctor will be of help in planning a schedule which will insure the proper nutrition for your child.

Our "built-in clocks and engines" shift and change without

regularity during childhood. Here again we must realize that each "clock" is different. For example, some infants can start on solid foods at two months. Others won't be ready until at least four or five months. Some infants thrive on what seems to be only milk. Others will prefer solids, and others may even have an allergy to milk and will require a substitute. Some children will let go of the bottle at eight months and others will hold onto it as though for dear life. I see nothing wrong in allowing such a child to continue having a night bottle even beyond the age of two. It is perfectly healthy, has a most tranquilizing effect on such children, and is nutritious as well.

Hitting the Bottle Again

Often children who have given up the bottle will ask for it again at a time of stress. This is frequently seen when another child comes into the family. Instead of frowning on the child's request and making any comment which would indicate your disapproval, it is healthier for you to realize that the child's needs are legitimate. He is frightened at being displaced and his sense of security is shaken. The bottle acts as a source of security, reminiscent of the child's being held, cuddled, and fed. An occasional bottle and affection and attention will hasten the departure of this transient need.

Problem Feeders, Not Eaters

The eating problems we see most often have their origin in the feeders, not the eaters. If it isn't the quantity that the mother is complaining about, it's the type of food the father finds fault with (but which the child relishes), or it may be manners that both mother and father find wanting. What should be the most natural event may turn out to be one where the child finally vomits or is unduly criticized and sent away from the table by an irate father. If this is the situation, you may be expecting too much too soon.

We must, as parents, adjust to a dining area where there will be spilled fluids and solids, children eating with fingers, the demand for a favorite spoon, glass or dish, noisy banter, slow eaters and fast eaters, poor eaters and good eaters, and food left over, even though it was a favorite dish the last time it was served. If a parent cannot become tolerant of these situations, then the problems faced at the dinner table are with the feeder, not the eater.

An Arena of Life

The eating area in the home is and should be an arena of life for the child. It is the place where the family can be together as a unit. It also becomes a battle arena for sibling rivalry. This is to be expected and dealt with—not avoided. Parents should expect it to be a place for give and take—at times for pleasant conversation or planning, at times for griping of sundry kinds by the children. It is noisy and should be lively. Then it is normal. I would feel there is something wrong if all were quiet, the strict authoritative figure sitting in "his" seat, every child knowing which fork to use at the proper time. Table manners among young children do not mean orderliness for the child. The edicts of Emily Post or Amy Vanderbilt are all right for the older teen-ager but are certainly never in order for young children.

And don't go worrying about "what will they think" while in a restaurant. Given their freedom at home around the table, we have never had cause to be embarrassed in a restaurant with any of our children. They readily accept the situation as different and respond with a change in behavior. I might add that this holds true for the respect a child shows towards other people's possessions. Having the freedom to do what they want with their toys, the boys' room will often look as though a tornado has ripped through it. Yet at other boys' homes, I've been told often how gentlemanly they are.

Noodging Not Needed

Mothers, and particularly grandmothers, often see children as malnourished. Given the opportunity, a child will eat what he needs. So don't noodge them to the point where they are under pressure and lose whatever appetite they have, or eat more than they need, only to vomit afterwards.

One of our children, who weighed the least at birth and

has always been on the thin side, eats more slowly and less than the others, yet appears to be less susceptible to many childhood illnesses. It is not uncommon that the child whom we think is the least nourished of all somehow has greater tolerance and resistance to many illnesses to which children are susceptible.

Sloppy Sleepers

It is on the first sleepless night that one realizes that a parent's life is not an easy one. We need our sleep, but most of our young children's sleeping patterns make it impossible. The cry, "For God's sake, go to sleep," is a universal one. And the thought, "Who needs this?" is there as well. Some children present no problem to the parents, but they are in the minority. At some time, in one way or another, most children will present some sleeping problems for their parents. Many are difficult to handle because they are a source of conflict between our own immediate needs for restful sleep and the needs of the child which do not permit it.

Children differ considerably in their need for sleep—how deeply they sleep, how restfully, and when they want their sleep. Below, I have listed the many sleeping problems I have encountered as a father and physician, with some means of remedying them. Some of you may look upon what I call "remedy" as no remedy at all. My criteria for remedy is a simple one. What is best for the healthy emotional growth of the child?

The Playboy

The playboy is the young child who goes to sleep peacefully enough but awakens during the night for a round of activities. Some children will go to the parents' bedroom and snuggle into bed with them. Others have their own ideas. It may be the late show on TV, some book or comics, perhaps a snack to be had in the kitchen. Some have been known to go outdoors and ring the neighbor's doorbell at 2 A.M. asking for the neighbor's dog. These are not the acts of a bad child who should therefore be punished. His needs may be strange to us but they are within the range of "normalcy," transient and troublesome to us for a short period.

If a child does something which he can handle himself, such as reading or eating, then provision can be made for him to do as he wants to. He will then return to sleep and probably wake none the worse for it. It is important with the playboy to see that he cannot injure himself.

The Wanderer

Some playboys become wanderers as well. They will find some means of getting out of the house and may take a tour of the neighborhood. This is dangerous as well as annoying to the neighbors. You must make sure that doors and windows are fastened for the night. But do not, I repeat, DO NOT fasten your child to his crib or bed. You may tie your dog, but never your child.

Several times I have been told of how the child when younger was "so terrible we had to tie him to his crib." One mother tied a net over the top. Another, less ingenious, tied the child's foot to the side of the crib. This should never be done.

Although the problem is a transient one, it can become a troublesome situation. If all else fails, it may become necessary to devise an alarm which informs you when your child wakes. Changing the child's bedtime or—in more severe cases—nighttime sedation, might be necessary, and should be discussed with the child's doctor.

The Town Crier

A cry is a form of expression. The child, unable to speak, expresses himself by crying. He may be uncomfortable, or hungry, or in pain, or just not tired enough for sleep. But there is something the child is trying to express. How much simpler it would be for all if he could talk and tell us! But he cannot. We must try to understand him. It can, I know from personal experience, be damned frustrating. So frustrating, in fact, that many a parent has slammed the door to the child's room and stomped out exclaiming, "I've had it!"—allowing a child to bellow even when neighbors would call to ask if anything was wrong. But frankly, I have never had the courage to do it. I have on several occasions sat in a darkened room and rocked a child or held my hand on his back, comforting him, with my wife standing outside whispering, "But they all say to let him cry it out . . ." I know that some pediatricians have recommended letting the child cry it out. In many cases it lasts just several nights. But in some cases I feel the parent will have to do as I did—remain awake and comfort the child.

The No-Nap Kid

The harried mother understandably welcomes the child's nap with a sigh of relief. It gives her a chance to do the many chores around the house which become quite difficult to handle with a toddler around. Here again there are vast differences among children. Some refuse to nap by their second birthday and don't seem to tire. Others still need a nap at five or six or they will show signs of fatigue and become grumpy in the later afternoon. Unless the no-nap child truly shows signs of weariness towards evening, mother will have to resign herself to a full active day and hope, at least, for a full night's sleep without interruption.

Room at the Side

Starting with the child's ability to climb out of the crib, there is a request for room at the side. It may be at the side of the mother or the father or in between. It can be persistent or occasional. It may be because of nightmares, or, more likely, a desire to hold on to mama at night as well as during the day. This practice must gently and firmly be stopped.

The simplest thing for the parent who is sleeping deeply is to continue sleeping. That is not the wisest thing to do. The child must learn that in bed mama belongs to papa and papa to mama and there is no room at the side, in the middle, beneath the bed, or on the floor next to the bed.

Where the child has entered the parents' bed, lifting him

and putting him back in his bed is the wisest, though at times more difficult, thing to do. Allowing him to sleep in the parents' bed is chancing disaster in later years. It is bad if we allow the child to associate the bed with either parent, for the bed in later years is associated with the sexual act. As a psychiatrist I have seen too many situations where a child's sleeping in bed with a parent was directly related to difficulties as a child and sexual difficulties in his adult years.

The Same Number of Stories, Please

Many normal children show a ritualistic behavior at bedtime which may seem bizarre to the parent. We are familiar with a child's frequent request to sleep with the same cuddly toy, often a teddy bear. Some children prefer other objects. Before falling peacefully asleep, many will insist on some exactly repeated procedure, such as tucking in the bed, performed by the same parent from the same side, the same cheek being kissed good night, *ad infinitum.*

It can be quite exasperating, but it is a legitimate need. If a child shows a tendency towards this behavior, limit the type and number of activities at bedtime to prevent a request for the same activities the next night.

The darkness, the unknown of sleep, is threatening to many children. "Will I wake up?" is a question the child repeatedly asks himself. The child seems to need rituals to maintain a semblance of control where, in fact, he feels he . has no control. It is a real need which must be accepted by the parents and should not be ridiculed. A firm, reassuring tone while doing the tucking-in or handing the cuddly toy to the child will do much to quiet his unspoken fears.

The Frightened One

Many children are fearful of the dark and of sleep. Often these fears are easily dealt with by simply allowing some light in the child's room. A child's mind is most imaginative. A simple shadow may be a lizard or a werewolf. To the child they are very real. It is, therefore, wrong to ridicule a child for having such fears. A sympathetic tone as you open the closet and show there is no Frankenstein monster there, or place your hand between the light and wall to show there is only a shadow, will help to reassure a child. We cannot deal effectively with a child's fear of the dark if we insist that the child think and feel as we do. Insisting that all lights be out, the door to the room shut, and that he not see the monster reminds me of an experience I had as a resident psychiatrist. A middle-aged woman responded to voices she "heard" and we recommended that she be committed for treatment to a state hospital. On the day of the court hearing for commitment, there sat an elderly judge who was most unsympathetic to recommendations by psychiatrists. He asked her about the voices she heard. She described in detail the messages she received from some statesmen on how to save the world. The judge listened, closed his eyes, and thought for a moment. Pointing his finger at her, he stated, "You're a fine woman, wanting to save the world. The doctors here say I have to send you away if you hear these things. But I'm going to send you home—only I don't want you to listen to these voices again."

A child's fears and imaginative fantasies are not the same as an adult's. They are normal for children, and telling them that they shouldn't see is as effective as telling psychotics with auditory hallucinations that they shouldn't listen.

Children, when frightened, will often insist that their parents lie next to them in bed. This need not be done. One can as readily comfort a child by standing over him or by sitting at the side of the bed. As I have mentioned above, lying in bed with a child can be emotionally harmful. It is a bad habit that should be avoided.

The Dreamer

We do not know why we dream. Recent research has shown that we all dream each night. Even infants and animals show evidence of dreaming. Some dreams are pleasant and the presence of some wish is evident. Other dreams are quite frightening to adult as well as child. The child, because of his limited life experiences, has more difficulty separating the real from the unreal, and is particularly vulnerable to being frightened by his dreams.

Children differ here as well. We know that all children dream, yet some are more disturbed than others by what they dream. Occasionally a child younger than five will awaken frightened, but it is usually after that age that a child finds himself disturbed. The child's screams at night can be quite frightening to the entire household. At times the child may have a night terror that makes it difficult to awaken him and comfort him. Realize that this is not unusual; the child will gradually calm down and return to sleep. Sitting at the bedside of the child to reassure him is essential. When he was seven one of my sons loved a particular television horror show. He would without fail have a nightmare after seeing the horror movie. When this pattern became evident I insisted that he not watch it—the show was too stimulating, too horrifying for him.

Whether dreams involve being chased by animals, Frankenstein's monster or the werewolf, it is important that parents accept them as one of the normal events in a child's development. Here again, a calm, reassuring parent is all that is necessary to overcome a transient disturbance.

The Early Bird

The early bird is a child who awakens at 6 A.M. and asks, "Where is everybody?" One can try having the child go to bed at a later hour, but often he is up again at the crack of dawn. If you are fortunate, toileting the child and handing him a plaything will keep him quiet for another hour, but usually someone will have to be up with him. It is far easier—and healthier for the child—if the parent adjusts to the child's needs rather than try to have the child adjust to the parent's needs. And it is fruitless to wish for someone like your neighbor's child, who sleeps till a later hour.

Toiling in the Toilet

Man has learned to soar through outer space, but he has yet to conquer inner space. It is lack of inner space in man which requires him to quickly get rid of waste his body does not need. Man has no means of conveniently storing his body waste. And so, not too long after eating and drinking, the child must rid himself of his urine and feces.

Just as the astronauts must toil with the burden of body waste, so each mother must toil in the toilet. When should the training begin so that the toiling finally ends?

Trained Mothers, Untrained Infants

Some parents during their child's early months can judge fairly accurately when the infant is about to have a bowel movement. What many fail to recognize is that the child is still untrained—the mother has merely trained herself. Many infants even on demand feeding have some regularity in the sequence of ingestion of food and elimination of waste. The mother may have simply trained herself to be aware of this regularity and then takes the proper measures for the child to conveniently deposit his waste. There is nothing wrong with this procedure if the mother is aware that the child is not really trained and is therefore blameless for any "accidents." The infant simply is not ready to be trained. When is he?

A Simple Question for a Complex System

Before we answer this simple question we are going to have to pay attention to a most complex apparatus—our nervous system.

Our nervous system consists of billions of cells in our brain and spinal cord and miles of "transmission lines" through which messages are relayed to all parts of our body. Our brain is more complex than all the computers in the world combined.

We are not born with our nervous system intact. As a child develops, more transmission lines are established, enabling a child to do such things as walk, talk, and use the muscles necessary for waste elimination. How fast these specific transmission lines are established varies with each individual. This accounts for one child learning to walk at ten months and another at seventeen months. A child may be speaking sentences at seventeen months and another will not do the same until twenty-four months. Yet both are quite normal. In similar fashion, one child may without difficulty be toilet trained at twenty-one months and another normal child may not be trained until later. It is simply that there are great variations in the time it takes for the nervous system to develop fully. The bladder when full sends a message to the brain to inform the child that he should urinate; or when the rectum is full the message is relayed to the brain that the child should defecate. This complex system takes time to develop and no amount of wishing or pressure will make it progress any faster. In fact, pressure will only impede the process because of emotional difficulties then secondarily developed by the child.

Toiling till Two

The nervous system usually is not ready for toilet training until twenty to twenty-four months of age. That is why we often find that children who are badgered to "perform" and children whose mother have "taken it easy" seem to develop toilet training at the same time. But there is a world of difference in the relationship established between the mother who badgers her child and the mother who "takes it easy."

When a child is pressured by words or feelings to perform on the potty before he is ready, the child feels the pressure and though he will, for the sake of the mother's love, begin to "control" himself, one can then expect difficulties in another area. The child may find it hard to sleep for fear of "losing control," or may show some difficulty at eating time. We psychiatrists have also seen emotional damage in adults, the victims of rigid toilet training, who have developed an enormous need for control in all areas of their lives. Far better to adjust the toilet training to a pace which is in keeping with the child's development.

The expenditure of energy and soiled diapers is far less costly than an emotional disturbance in your child.

Do Not Flush!

I am sometimes amazed at how far some mothers will go to achieve bowel training. One mother I knew was quite bright, yet apparently had no awareness that what she was doing was wrong for her child. Emil was six months old that summer and the mother loved the beach. So she gave Emil a rectal suppository each morning and put him on some contraption attached to the toilet seat. This was to insure his evacuating all stool—and no mess at the beach. But Emil was a frail six months and his muscles were not yet developed so that he could sit properly on the contraption. Still, the mother felt she had overcome a mess at the beach until one day she heard a whimpering from the bathroom. There was little Emil Jack-knifed like a V in the toilet bowl, his rump in the water and his eyes staring at his toes.

Having a Potty

The advantage of having a potty for toilet training outweighs its disadvantages. It may not be as sanitary and it takes up more room; at times it stinks and it must be cleaned. But it is the right size and the child can sit comfortably on it with his feet on the floor while learning one of the rudiments of living in a civilized society. Also, it makes no noise, as does the toilet, into which a child sees a part of himself being devoured and disappearing. I know this sounds ridiculous to some parents, yet this is what we sometimes hear from children who have difficulty in using a toilet.

I've Got a Secret

Richard was seven years old when I was consulted because he was soiling himself when home. At school he would reluctantly use the toilet, and also when visiting friends or away from home. He was a handsome, charming, and bright seven-year-old. But with his pants full of feces the parents lost sight of the positive side. After several sessions he revealed that he often saw mother seated on the toilet and he knew "a secret." It later developed that his mother never troubled herself to close the door to the bathroom, performing her bodily functions in full view of Richard. At first she did so in order to keep an eye on him and in later years it became a "habit."

Richard became aware of a difference between his genitals and his mother's. In his eyes, mother merely had hair but no genitals. He associated her lack of a penis with sitting on the toilet and flushing it away. This was his secret! Here is another good example of how a child's mind works. What he saw happen to feces he felt could happen to his penis— particularly when he saw his mother rise from a sitting position minus a penis.

U. F. O.

Some parents become concerned when they see their infant playing with a bowel movement. They need not be. Many children like to absorb this marvelous production of theirs They smell it, finger it, and even taste it. One way to prevent this is to be aware of the approximate hour of a bowel movement, and soon after the bowel movement make the necessary changes.

When I was a medical student at Bellevue Hospital, the problem of a child playing with feces was brought to my attention quite vividly. One day on entering the pediatric ward I heard the shout, "Duck, duck!" Too late. My colleague and I were spattered with brown spots on our neat white doctors' coats. For a moment it didn't dawn on either of us what it was or where it came from. The intern who shouted at us to duck laughingly apologized for one of the children, who playfully threw his B.M.'s whenever he saw white.

Where Is It?

Another exasperating experience for parents is the child who defecates and then hides it. Or the child who defecates in some corner or closet. A hunt begins. Where is it? I think I smell it. But for the odor and inconvenience, it is not a serious problem. It is fairly common and transient. It is a child's nonverbal means of telling you that for some reason he doesn't want to part with his malodorous accomplishment.

An Ancient Laundry Problem

Bed-wetting in children beyond the age of four is a problem which has plagued many children and their parents for many centuries. Egyptian papyri have been found on which was inscribed a remedy, a local herb mixture. Thousands of years and millions of bed-wetters later, we are still unable to find a simple cause or a simple remedy.

I have known of some children who were bed-wetters in their late teens. I recall the many naval medical board meetings I attended while on duty as a psychiatrist in the navy. Many a recruit was brought to our attention for wetting his bunk at night. We had little choice but to give them an administrative discharge. Sadly, on enlisting, many confided their plight to a recruiting officer only to be told not to mention it again until they were in training camp because we in the navy had some magical potion that would cure them. I wish it were true.

During my training as a psychiatrist, the tendency was to view this problem as sheerly emotional—that is to say, stemming from some unconscious need or conflict. There may be a genetic influence. In a majority of cases brought to my attention, a thorough medical history revealed that either one or both parents had a history of nighttime wetting.

On several occasions children brought for consultation for other problems gave a history of bed-wetting. When I told this to the parents, they felt it was no emotional problem at all, pointing out that they had had a similar problem. One mother laughingly told how, when she was a teen-ager, her mother asked her, "Who is going to want to marry a girl who wets her bed at night?"

"At least I stopped on my honeymoon," she laughingly declared as she glanced at her husband. He quickly nodded agreement.

Most bed-wetting problems happily taper off between the ages of seven and nine. During the most troublesome years it presents a serious problem for the child who is shamed for what he has done. I am more concerned about the emotional harm it may inflict on some children than the laundry problem it presents to the mother. If mothers could learn to more readily accept this problem and impart this acceptance to the other children in the family, the child would feel much less different and less ashamed. It would also help if mother would not swathe the older child with diapers, but would allow him to wear normal pajamas, and use rubber or plastic sheets to protect the mattress or pillow.

Singling out the child for ridicule and shame will not make matters any easier. Making him aware that he should urinate just before going to bed and limiting his water intake after dinner will help.

Some parents like to awaken the child and carry him half asleep to the bathroom. This can worsen the situation, as he may unconsciously feel some gain from this extra attention. I would also suggest that if a parent feels it should be done, the parent of the same sex as the child perform the chores.

Some doctors recommend the use of a drug, Imipramine hydrochloride, and report favorable results, others recommend a conditioning device, activated by moisture, which signals to the child that he is wetting. Some children respond to such devices and are dry after a few weeks.

Where the problem is not a nightly one, the extra motivation involved in being fully accepted can be put into use. A number of children I have seen in my practice have after going to summer camp been completely dry. Should this occur only to reoccur in the home, a situation in the family relationship at home must be looked into.

A Step Backwards

When something traumatic happens to a child we often find that he regresses; he takes a step back in this development. He may begin wetting and soiling himself again after he is trained. Most often it is transient, such as after the birth of another child. When it seems to become fixed, then professional help must be sought.

Soiling After Three

We normally expect that the child be trained for bowel movements before he is fully trained for bladder control. Where bowel training has not been attained after three, and where it has been attained and lost, the child has a problem which should be discussed with your pediatrician.

Goodbye Mama, Goodbye Papa

There comes a time when a child must learn to say calmly, "Goodbye mama, goodbye papa," and be able to leave those whose very presence means love and security. Here, too, there are marked differences as to how each child reacts to the normal demands of separation. Some may lie in their cribs drinking their bottles, only to fling the bottle aside and begin to wail as mother steps out of sight. Others placidly accept separation, whether for an hour or longer.

During the first several months of life, the child's life centers around food, sleep, and elimination. If he is held securely and comfortably, it matters little to the infant who does the holding, the feeding, and the changing of diapers. This changes at about six months. He gradually becomes very much aware of the one who does most of the caring for him. We see it quite strongly at nine months. The child has begun to feel himself as an entity. In fact, he has become a little person who now relates and communicates more readily with those about him. The father feels this and will respond in turn. This is unlike some weeks before when the child showed little interest in his father.

The bonds between people, as we know them in adulthood, are becoming much stronger as the child relates to the people around him and they respond to him. As these bonds develop the child begins to feel a marked dependency. Though varying in intensity, it should be shown by all children. Your child feels helpless and relates in a manner which says, "Unless I have you [and to have is to see to the child] I cease to exist." Do we want such an intense feeling of helplessness and dependency to develop? Yes. At this time it is both necessary and desirable for the child's development. We, as parents, have become a most important stepping stone to the outside world.

There Is No One, I Am No One

We can readily see the harm that befalls those unfortunate children who are institutionalized and have had no true mother substitute. They withdraw into themselves. They seem to stop functioning as people—because people communicate. If we were to summarize their feelings, they would be saying, "There is no one, and I am no one."

It's Always Hello Before Goodbye

How is it that in a chapter which begins by stating that a child must learn to be separated from his parents, I go on to advocate the necessity of just the opposite—dependency? There is a simple answer. Before we can say goodbye, we have to say hello. In other words, there is an exchange. It is an exchange not only of words but of feelings as well. Our hello to our children should have several meanings. It should say, "I love you. I accept you. I will protect you and you are safe with me." But it should not end just there. It should go on to say, "I have confidence in you as an individual. I want you to grow up and become free and independent." The hello of the child says, "I can trust you. You love me and I love you. I am secure with you. You will be there when I need you."

With this exchange of feeling the child can then go on to the next stage in this area of development and in due time be able to say, "Goodbye mama, goodbye papa."

Goodbye at Three

At the age of about three most children are able to understand that parents do return after leaving them, though the dreadful feeling of abandonment can be quite strong in some children. Again we see marked differences in children. The differences may not be related to the relationship that has developed, consciously or unconsciously, between mother and child. It may simply be a matter of greater sensitivity to separation. And we must pay attention to the child's needs because they are based on very real fears. Some children need a longer exchange of reassurance.

Shoehorns Often Help

Sometimes our feet glide easily into new shoes and sometimes we need a shoehorn. So it is with children in new situations. Take nursery school or kindergarten, for example. Some children smilingly wave goodbye and enter the new relationship with relish. Others cling to their mothers as though holding on to dear life itself.

This can usually be avoided if "shoehorns" are used early. Many children between the ages of three and four will gradually take to a play group which can be organized by mothers. All mothers and children can play together at first, then perhaps two mothers, and finally one mother can stay with three to six youngsters for an hour (or perhaps two, if the number of children is kept low).

Nursery school is another valuable experience for many youngsters. If properly equipped and run, a child of four is more able to tolerate separation in an interesting and stimulating environment. I have observed that a strong motivating factor for my children to attend nursery school has been their desire to attend a school like their older brothers. They clearly felt it gave them status in the family. They, too, could come home and talk about the pets and interesting projects at nursery school.

Some Shoehorns

Children who have not had the experience of a play group and show separation anxiety on entry into nursery school or kindergarten can be helped in the following ways:

1—Stay with the child for the whole first day, or for several days if necessary.

2—Make certain you are on time when school lets out, or at home if the child returns by car or bus.

3—Enlist the aid of your child's teacher, who in all likelihood has had experience with such difficulties.

4—Enlist the aid of a classmate of your child who does not show separation anxiety. A buddy system will often work.

5—Continue to reassure the child. Shaming the child, or yelling, will only aggravate the situation.

Camping Trials and Trails

Camp during the summer is a wonderful chance for the child to say "goodbye mama, goodbye papa." A well-run day camp for younger children (five through eight) is a good experience and at nine or older a sleep-away camp should be considered. (Again, each child is unique—some can easily leave for an eight-week stay at an earlier age, particularly if an older brother or relative or friend accompanies them.)

If you are financially able, having your child attend a summer sleep-away camp has several distinct advantages.

1—It enables him to form a sense of independence and to be able to feel he can enjoy life without having his parents close by.

2—There will be an opportunity for more give and take with his peers when he lives with them twenty-four hours a day, seven days a week.

3—It gives him a feeling of freedom from the demands made upon him by school and parents.

4—It enables him to pursue activities he likes (hopefully the camp is so run).

5—It gives the parents a needed respite.

And let us not belittle this need of parents, who also need a rest from the tumultuous world of children. This brings up the matter of:

A Plea for Individualism

Too much has been said and done about the idea of togetherness. Yes, I recommend togetherness when eating, but I don't recommend it for the bathroom—nor for long vacations. Parents often err in taking along a teen-ager to a resort, not considering that there may not be another teen-ager there. The child is miserable and lonely and the parents are angry at such ingratitude. What should the child be thankful for? Loneliness?

Some parents take along a station-wagon-load of children for a trip across the continent. Many miles and rest rooms later, it is evident that a mistake has been made. It's too late to turn back and you wish you could "drop the load" and are even willing to go back to work. When we consider that each child has his own emotional needs at any given age, it becomes obvious that it is often impossible to meet those needs by hitting upon some magical average that will take care of everyone and leave him content. Better to consider the needs of each than to put them into a group and hope for the best. It is wrong for us to insist that our children yield to our needs. As parents we must consider *their needs*. On vacation we may need to relax in the sun or visit a museum or gallery. They may need to go swimming or catch some lizards. If you're willing to yield, then going with them can be pleasurable, but if you insist that they yield mostly to your needs, a mess of hard feelings is sure to follow.

It's His Choice

Much of camp life in the past was occupied with physical activities. Today there are camps whose many activities deal with each child as an individual, as they should. There are children who are more athletically inclined than others. If they prefer to be on a baseball diamond all day, that is perfectly all right. There are children who would prefer to go on an "archeological expedition" and find some artifacts. This is fine. It is preposterous to insist that a child who prefers to read or look into a microscope should be on the baseball diamond because "that's where most of the boys are." Or to insist that a girl join the art group when she prefers the volleyball court.

Choose a camp that has the activities that your child prefers—*not* what you prefer or think your child *should* prefer.

I Wanna Come Home

Not infrequently a child refuses to go away to camp, or once there writes or calls in desperation to come home at once. Often the pendulum of emotions swings so quickly and frequently that parents who rush up to camp to rescue their child are confronted by a child who looks at them with puzzlement when they ask, "What's wrong?" "Where?" the child has been known to respond.

Should he persist in his demand to return home it is most likely a matter of difficulty in being separated from you, not of maltreatment at camp.

If the child is nine or older and the only difficulty is homesickness, have him remain and learn to endure separation. In several instances I have seen the difficulty of remaining at camp, saying "goodbye mama, goodbye papa," become more fixed. Years later, going off to an out-of-town college becomes a serious problem. Here again the "shoehorns" I have mentioned, with some modification, will be of help.

1—Though the child may find it embarrassing, remain in the locality for a day or two while he gets a further chance to adjust.

2—Enlist the aid of a mature counselor who has handled such problems.

3—If the child has shown separation difficulty in the past or is apprehensive about camp, have him go with a close friend or relative he likes. There is strength in unity, and a buddy system helps either before he goes or once he is there.

4—It is important that on visiting days parents be there without fail.

Dear Parents. . . .

The quick shift in feelings and the free language of the nine-year-old are so beautifully illustrated by some letters a mother laughingly showed me, that I prevailed upon her to allow me to publish them. The following two letters were sent by her very normal nine-year-old son on the second day of his first trip to a sleep-away camp. His mother received them both together and opened them in the apparent order in which they were sent. A further note of explanation: The first letter was quickly inserted in an envelope for mailing as the counselor approached the boy to see what was being done. A rule of the camp was that letters be screened by the counselor.

Okay—Come Home

If all is tried and the child remains adamant, then agree to have the child return home. Planning for another chance the following year, perhaps with a friend, would be a good idea.

Dear family,
        This camp is turning to s——,
because 3 f——— are teasing me;
I don't like to be teased. They are
calling me pandy bear. They
are singing Andy Pandy put ten
in a pie, kissed the girls and
made 'em cri. They say that
all the time. They tease me
about my hair cream, they say
it smells; I want to go home
now, rite away. If they stay for
eight weeks I am staying for four,
and the other way. For Daddy
I don't want to laugh it off, and
I don't want to live with some
f——— who have promblems, and
need a sigiagrest, Dont worry I
wasnt caught

Dear Mom,

You letter send up the lumeris paint. Not on visiting day. Please send up the lumeris paint as soon as you get the letter.

Please send up more stamps. I am always lending stamps to my friend.

I just made friends with may enimies.

Camp is great. I am having a good time.

This is the third day of camp and still needs stiff to do. Camp has only swimming, baseball, and free periods. Please send up more envolopes.

Love Andy

Threatening Habits

During the normal course of maturation, because of unavoidable stresses and strains, many children develop habits which, though temporary and quite harmless, threaten many parents into statements and acts which do little to stop the habits, and often cause further difficulties.

These habits appear to threaten us into feeling there is something mentally wrong with our children, that perhaps we have done something wrong in raising them—we are afraid that everyone can see that something is wrong with us and our children.

The fact is that in most cases there is no need to have such fears at all. Let us take a look at such habits as thumbsucking, head banging, biting, teeth clicking, tongue rolling, ear tugging, nose picking, head rolling, hair tugging, eye blinking, nail biting, and stuttering.

Damn Yankers

How would we like to have a newly lit cigarette yanked out of our mouths? Or a foul-tasting substance put on the filter tip? Or have some fiendish-looking metal rake attached to our teeth so that it chomps off the cigarette tip? Sounds foolish and not very pleasant. Yet this is what some of us do to our children when we find them sucking their thumbs. We become damn yankers.

As adults, we are aware of the pressures we must live with. So some of us like to take a coffee break, other like to light up a cigarette, cigar, or pipe. We do so even at the risk of lung cancer. Yet let one of our little ones show some signs of tension by putting his thumb in his mouth and we become frantic. Why? What is it about a child's thumb in his mouth that threatens us? Children, no matter what age, live with anxieties and tensions like our own. In our adult lives many of the anxieties and tensions are unavoidable. This is true of our children as well. Tensions are painful and when these tensions build up, we—adults as well as children—seek some means of gratification to offset the pain. That gratification, in many of us, is gained by the use of our mouths. In the language of psychiatry, we seek oral gratification.

Thumbsucking usually starts within the first several months. After being fed, the child continues to seek for the pleasurable feeling associated with the feeding. There is nothing wrong. Later the child will seek the thumb before meals as well. He may also thumbsuck when tired and frustrated. At times we can know what the signal of thumb-sucking means and take the necessary measures to relieve the tension. At other times there is unavoidable frustration. The important thing is not to become worried about either emotional implications or poor teeth formation. The habit is harmless in almost all cases and will run its natural course and will eventually stop.

That Wondrous Head

Not only does the head have a mouth with which to suck and eat, it also has a world of appendages to the child. It has a tongue which can be twisted and sucked, teeth which can bite and be ground, eyes which can blink, ears which can be tugged, a nose which can be picked, and hair which can be curled, twisted, and pulled. And, using everything, one can make a funny face.

Clothes-Chewers

Some children will hold onto some soft clothing or toy while sucking a thumb. At times a thumb is replaced by a twisted collar, or a piece of shirt or dress. This can be quite trou-blesome to the mother and father. It not only looks grotesque but is costly as well. Fortunately, it too stops. While it continues one can attempt to understand the conditions which cause it and tackle the cause rather than the effect we see. Try not to criticize the child. Certainly no punishment is indicated. The latter will only aggravate the condition and you will have a vicious cycle of

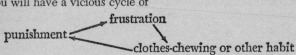

In similar fashion this vicious cycle can be set in motion with any of the habits of children we parents find unpleasant.

Let Go!

It is not uncommon for a group of mothers in a play area to be startled by the cry, "Let go!" Turning about they see the smallest of the group holding onto a real meaty one with the most tenacious grip of "baby" teeth. In all likelihood the small one, frustrated in his efforts at play, resorts to the only form of aggression which will inflict pain on his larger adversaries. Happily the child grows—his feet to kick, his hands to punch, and speech to communicate better. In the meantime one must consider removing the little biter from situations which foster such actions. At times this is difficult, as in an elevator, where the little biter's face is in close contact with a rotund backside. What can one do? Just be relieved when the elevator comes to your floor.

Nail-Nibblers

Nail-nibbling presents a more difficult problem than thumbsucking because in some children it persists in later years. Many of us know friends who continue to chew on their nails when they are under pressure. Once I had referred the mother of a child I was treating to a colleague. She called to tell me how disappointed she was. Her main argument was summed up as follows.

"Have you seen his hands? Why, he bites his fingernails so badly that he must be awfully anxious himself."

Yes, it is true that some anxiety must be the basis for nail-nibbling. But as parents, if we harangue the child to stop or put some bitter substance on the nail, we can then be starting the vicious cycle I have shown above. Far better to seek to relieve as many causes of tension as possible. Often teen-agers stop nibbling in adulthood—particularly girls who want to keep their hands looking pretty.

Waiting for the Word

Speech is a complicated process which makes man different from all other animals. During the development of speech there will normally occur in children some sporadic difficulties in speaking clearly. They will repeat sounds, parts of words, and whole words. Many children have this difficulty at one time or another so that we can consider this a normal event in speech maturation. It should not be called stuttering, which it really is not. Nor should the child be criticized, or, in fact, any fuss at all be made when the child is expressing himself. Instead, calmly listen to all he has to say without telling him to "slow down," and don't ask that something be repeated because you felt it wasn't expressed clearly. Don't talk, just listen.

The Eyes Have It

Another concern of parents is when the child's tension is manifested by blinking eyes. Here again the majority of cases are transient, harmless episodes. I have observed this mostly in boys, particularly between six and nine years of age. Try not to pay attention to it and do not have the child become concerned or you will find an increase in the very habit you are trying to stop.

Rock, Bang, and Roll

Rock and roll is not limited to teen-agers. It is not uncommon to find children who show one or more habits of rocking, banging their heads, or rolling their heads. These, too, will run their course and are nothing to become alarmed about. Many children rock themselves to sleep. Some of them are head-bangers as well. Usually they are aggressive, assertive children who really clobber their heads hard against some door, particularly when frustrated and angry. Fatigue can lead to it, so a nap may be in order. The danger here, of course, is injury to the forehead. You can prevent that by quickly getting to the child as he starts his head-banging tirade. Children who roll their heads are rarer. Fortunately, all these habits quietly fade away. We must be patient.

Twirlers, Curlers, and Pullers

Some children discover that hair is a wonderful thing to hold onto when they are anxious or frustrated. Merely twirling and curling of the hair is sufficient for some. Others are not content with simply twirling, they pull at it as well and bald spots begin to appear. Here my experience has been that it is not a simple habit that will spontaneously disappear. It may also be that all the children with self-caused baldness were brought to my attention for treatment. Perhaps there had been spontaneous improvement in others. In any event, pulling to a point of baldness is usually indicative of a more severe conflict which requires professional help.

Genitally Speaking

As children develop, it is only normal for them to become aware of the various parts of their bodies. They learn that some parts are more sensitive than others and that these areas give pleasure when touched. Every child at one time or another will quite naturally touch or stroke the genitals which are the most sensitive parts of the body. This appears to disturb some parents to the point of looking at their child as some precocious sexual monster. Let me assure every parent that the touching and stroking of the genitals in young children is quite normal. We observe its onset in children between the first and second years.

Never!

I recall a session in a child development class when a group of us were observing children from the time of their birth through their childhood years. We were speaking with a mother while her nude one-year-old boy lay nearby on an examining table. The boy was putting his hand on his penis only to have his mother pull it away. This occurred several times, and one of the doctors asked the mother, "How long has it been since you've noticed your son playing with his penis?"

"Why, Doctor, he never has done any such thing!" was her quick response.

It was quite apparent that the idea of her son doing "any such thing" was repellent to the woman. She was actually not fully conscious of her own act of pulling her son's hand away

49

from his genitals. Certainly this was not a thing the mother had to deny or become concerned about. Yet all too often the feelings, statements, and acts of overly concerned parents do as much harm to children as those parents who are too liberal in the area of sex. There is a solid middle ground that we should attempt to stand upon.

Let us see what is is normal and what is not, when to say something and when to say little or nothing, when to take some action and when no action is necessary.

Show and Do Not Tell

Just as it is normal for the young child to begin to explore and touch parts of his body, so it is normal for children to sometimes compare their genitals and girls their breasts. Here, again, let us realize that such activity is within normal limits of curiosity. Brothers, for example, will at times compare the size of their penises, which to them have become the most important appendages on their bodies. Should the parents find young children in a partial stage of undress playing "doctor," a simple comment that such activity is not necessary is sufficient. Threats and punishment are quite unnecessary.

Once my wife, during her teaching days, was amazed to see a friend and colleague leading two partially disrobed boys with their hands over their heads to the principal's office. Her friend explained heatedly that she had found the two nine-year-olds in a clothes closet with their pants open comparing penis sizes. They were soon joined by another teacher and reason prevailed—the boys were allowed to zip up their pants and return to their class.

Blindness, Insanity, and Hell

Children to this day are wrongfully warned that the touching of the genitals will lead to blindness, some are told that they will go insane, and some Catholics I have seen were told that they would go to hell. I wish that those who have made such warnings could see the young people who bear emotional scars because of this nonsense they have been told.

Excessive Genital Play

There are children who, for one reason or another, have much anxiety and as a result will masturbate excessively. These children are in need of help, as was one eight-year-old boy whose mother asked for a consultation. The chief complaint was that the teacher informed the mother that she noticed his hand in his pocket moving over the genital area. He continually stroked his genitals while occupied with his schoolwork.

His history revealed that prior to the onset of this habit the boy's father had suffered a severe heart attack. He was hospitalized and much talk at home centered around his survival. The boy was, unfortunately, brought into these conversations. It was also unfortunate that a relative had turned to him and said, "You're the man around the house while Dad isn't here. You're strong and can take care of mother and Emmy [his little sister]."

The child was terribly frightened and his excessive masturbation was directly related to his fear. Where there is excessive masturbation the cause of anxiety must be dealt with. It is the anxiety which leads to the masturbation. Admonitions and punishment are not the answer to the difficulty.

Handwriting on the Wall

Another normal occurrence in the difficult process of growing up, particularly in boys, is the matter of using obscene words, both spoken and written. Parents often react with unwarranted concern and, at times, unwarranted punishment. A firm hand may sometimes be needed, but certainly not on the child's buttocks. And washing a child's mouth with soap (a not-so-rare procedure even today) is a terrible and really unjustifiable act.

A Penmanship Lesson

At the age of four most boys and girls take great delight in using "dirty words," usually scatological. We seem better able to tolerate such words as "Do-do" and "Noo-noo" accompanied by a child's laughter. But when at age six, and thereafter, the four- and five-letter words associated with sex start being used and written, some of us get a little shaken. I, too, was taken aback when suddenly one day I heard a repetitive cry of "f---." "Now where did he hear that?" I asked myself. The answer was simple. It has occurred with millions of other children. My son, then seven, had simply heard it said by an older boy whom he had admired that week. But I wasn't quite prepared for what happened next.

Many children (and sadly, some adults) use the walls for a more permanent display of their new-found knowledge. After all, the echo of a verbal expression doesn't last long enough. My son preferred to make a four-letter word into a penmanship lesson. There in neat rows of twenty-five lines on the sheet was written "f---." My wife, on seeing it, decided to put her foot down. (Here again, as angry and frustrated as we may be, use the floor and not the child.) As she related the incident to me, she told him never to use the word again.

"But S. and D. use it all the time. What's so terrible about it?" was his protest.

She repeated, "It's not a nice word. I don't want to see or hear you use it again."

"Tell me why it's not nice. What does it mean?" he asked again.

As a modern mother she found herself on a tightrope. On the one hand she wanted to stop the use of the word, and on the other hand she didn't want him to associate sex with something bad. She thought awhile and told him that the way it was being used, it was often used in a bad way, but what it means was not bad—it had to do with a mother and father getting together so that they could have a baby.

"Is that all?" he asked.

About a half hour later two friends came calling to play soccer, and he could clearly be heard saying to both, "Hi, S.—Your mother had two f---s. And D.—your mother had three f---s." The number of children in each family! Of course, this was not expected, but apparently it did the trick. Since then we have not heard the word bandied about.

Growing Pains

As parents we have no choice but to share in the growing pains of our children. The use of obscene words is one of many growing pains. It comes at a time when a child is torn between feeling and wanting his independence, and realizing that he is still dependent. It is a time when boys no longer look up to their fathers and think they are the greatest. This comes as a blow to many fathers. The apple of his eye, who pleaded with him only a year ago to take him wherever he went, now prefers the company of his friends. He not only likes to use the words his friends use but wants to wear the same kind of shoes, hair style, etc. No longer does he appear to emulate his "square" father, but imitates his friends. But make no mistake regarding our influence as parents. We are, of course, and should continue to be, very much there Striving as they do to meet the world as independent beings, children continue to feel their need for us They will, in the long run, be influenced by us more than we realize.

Birds, Bees, and Parents Too

We all agree that it is important for us to be honest with our children, yet many of us find it difficult to be honest with our children when it comes to sexual education. Many parents have great difficulties when it comes to answering the normal questions of a curious child. Some children are still told that a stork brought them or that they were bought at a "Baby Store." A young child's questions about birth and sex are to him like the questions he might have about where food comes from. Or how it is made. It would help all of us if we could learn to be simple, honest, and direct in our answers.

Why Do You Ask?

There is no simple stock answer we can give all our children. Circumstances, such as a pregnancy in a family member or a pet, the age of a child, the degree of inquisitiveness, will vary from child to child.

Perhaps you have heard the story of how Jimmy's father, on being asked, "Where did I come from?" began to go into a long dissertation on love and marriage. Jimmy, eight, interrupted his father with a quizzical look and repeated, "Where did *I* come from? Tommy said *he* came from Chicago."

It would have helped if Jimmy's father knew why Jimmy was asking the question. Here a simple question, "Why do you ask?" can be of value in eliciting the reason for the questions. You can then be informed as to what your child has been thinking, or perhaps has been told elsewhere, and go on from there.

We need not feel under pressure to tell more than is necessary at a particular age and time. The experience of two of my friends can well illustrate this point.

Seeds Are for Gardens

One spring day Larry saw the gardener sprinkling grass seeds on the lawn. Being a bright and inquisitive five-year-old, he began to ask the gardener what he was doing. On being informed that he was putting "seeds on the lawn," Larry ran into the house and exclaimed to his mother, "Tony is throwing his seeds on the ground. Shouldn't he be putting them in your vagina?"

All too frequently an analogy at this age is too complex for the child to comprehend. Larry's questions regarding where a neighbor's newborn came from could have been simply answered, "It grew in his mother's abdomen"—or the word "tummy" can be used. The word "stomach" is not recommended for several reasons. It can present you with the difficulty of trying to explain how a stomach can be used for both food and childbearing. Anatomically, the word "abdomen" is correct. At a later time the word "uterus" can be introduced and its enlargement into the abdominal cavity explained.

Silly Rules

Frequently we find ourselves saying more than is necessary when we unconsciously and consciously try to interject morality into a simple answer to a young child's questions. A friend's wife, when asked by her six-year-old daughter, "Does a woman need a man to have a baby?" responded, "Yes, when they are married."

Little Esther looked puzzled, "Why do they have to be married?" she asked.

"Because those are the rules."

The brief dialogue ended as little Esther walked away muttering, "You make up such silly rules."

Simple anatomical and physiological knowledge has nothing whatsoever to do with morality. Most children through the age of seven are content with a simple explanation that a baby grows in the mother's abdomen. Some may ask where it comes out. The answer is, "Through a special opening." You can always put a stop to a more direct detailed question such as, "Can you show me the opening?" The answer is a firm, unembarrassed "No. This is one of the things you will learn about a woman's body as you grow older."

Sometimes at eight, and more commonly at nine and ten, more specific questions are raised regarding the man's role. At this age a child is more readily able to grasp the idea that a man deposits "something like a seed" and it joins together with a tiny egg somewhere in mother's abdomen. The tiny egg is then able to grow for nine months and comes out through a special opening near where urine comes out. At this age it is unnecessary to go into a long explanation of loving and caring for one another. It will, at this time, make little sense to the child. A simple, forthright, unemotional answer by the mother or father is all that is needed.

Schools have happily taken on more of the responsibility of sex education. This is good because in some cases it can supplement what is learned at home, and—where the parents have too great a difficulty handling the questions—the school can do the proper educating. In some areas pediatricians and doctors have groups of youngsters for sessions on sex education. This is extremely valuable, particularly when menstruation and nocturnal emission have to be explained. Clear scientific language and anatomical diagrams can be used in an atmosphere devoid of embarrassment and ignorance. This should be accomplished some months in advance of a girl's first menstrual period. Girls can be made to feel proud that they are attaining womanhood and their bodies are preparing for motherhood. There is no place for such phrases as the "monthly curse." Have a mother indicating through the years her dread of menstruation, and you are certain to have a daughter with problems.

Ignorance and the Unconscious

Cynthia not only had to contend with her mother—her grandmother added greatly to the conflicts her mother had already stirred up within her.

She could recall that as a child of eight she was exposed to her grandmother's comments regarding sex as befitting animals only. And since grandfather wanted his sex, he was the "animal." Cynthia had her first menses before the age of twelve. She was totally unprepared and thought she had somehow injured herself. Running tearfully she encountered her grandmother, who laughingly slapped her face. Puzzled, she ran to her mother who likewise slapped her face (where does this barbaric ritual stem from?) and congratulated her. Congratulations for what? She was now aware she had the "monthly curse." All she could do was cry.

Within months, bosoms enlarged, hips became more rounded, and the mother took over the grooming process. Many months before other girls in her class were using makeup and wearing tight sweaters, Cynthia was—on mother's subtle urgings. Cynthia's mother had been married to a man she barely knew, all prearranged by her parents. Unhappy in her marriage, she began using her daughter, quite unconsciously, and derived vicarious gratification from her daughter's tales of dating and petting. Reared in ignorance, and now somehow urged on without understanding why, Cynthia found herself in need of help. It was quite a dilemma. Sex was both dirty and somehow urged upon her. What was the right thing to do? In treatment Cynthia spoke of how she felt mother somehow urging her on and could still hear her grandmother calling grandfather "the animal."

It would have been far healthier had Cynthia been prepared for her menses, had adequate knowledge of sex, and developed pride in her body and its womanly function. Of course, it would have also been much healthier for her if her grandmother had not confided her difficulties and if her mother had not derived erotic pleasure from Cynthia's sexual encounters. It is not uncommon for a girl to find herself in difficulty because of ignorance and to become promiscuous to please her own mother's unconscious desires! This may shock some parents, yet this is what sometimes happens.

Infant Casanovas

Shock, embarrassment, anger, concern are but a few of the feelings we parents have as our children develop sexually. These feelings are particularly seen in parents who are faced with the realization that their young child not only manifests an interest in sex but is so precocious as to attempt an overt sexual act. Often the chosen partner is a sibling or parent. A firm, disapproving action must be taken. Where it is hinted or known that a brother and sister are involved in some hanky-panky, it is necessary to state firmly that such action is forbidden. Closer supervision and physical separation at bedtime then becomes essential. Sharing the same bedroom is to be avoided. Such goings-on need not cause undue alarm or result in any punishment. Nor should the child be belittled nor the matter brought to the attention of other members of the family.

Often a harsh reaction from a parent can inflict harm which lasts for many years. I am reminded of the episode told to me by Mr. K. E. A tall, handsome man of forty, I saw him briefly prior to his accepting a new position in a distant state. He came seeking help after years of suffering with chronic anxiety. Whenever he had to talk to an employer or official he would become very upset, his forehead and hands would perspire, he could feel his heart pounding and he felt faint. In the several sessions which followed our first interview, he spoke at length about his childhood, years filled with terror of his father. Unlike what we see in Hollywood films, it is not usual that a troubled individual can trace his difficulties to one traumatic episode. But Mr. E. could vividly describe what he felt to be the episode which, as he phrased it, "seemed to set the basis for the feelings we [i.e., father and son] had for

58

each other." He went on, "I remember I was just six. I had just gotten up to go to the bathroom. I took off my pajamas and walked into my parents' bedroom. I remember holding my penis and talking to my mother. I was saying something about the penis and her. The next thing I remember is my father giving me one terrific wallop across my head. I remember his screaming at me something like, 'You little bastard. Who do you think you are?'—all the time smashing me across the face." With a visible shudder he ended, describing the scene with, "I'll never forget that morning."

It would be incorrect to say that this alone was cause for Mr. E.'s difficulties. Yet he was correct in saying, "(it) seemed to set the basis for the feelings we had for each other." Such comments by his father as "You'll never be half the man I am," reinforced Mr. E.'s sense of inadequacy. His father also reminded him of the scene, reinforcing the anger Mr. E. felt towards him, and, unconsciously, towards all authority figures.

No Need To Be Shocked

It is untrue that sexual feelings come only with the biological ability to procreate. They are present years before the boy's body is physically capable of sperm production or the girl's body capable of bearing a child.

And do not be shocked by expressions of sexual feelings from children. Sometimes their rich fantasy life can be quite disconcerting to themselves, the parent, and others. For example, one normal eight-year-old girl returned home to inform her parents that while at her playmate's home that day, her friend's father "molested" her. Irate and filled with rage her parents made some phone calls. Fortunately the situation did not get out of hand—it was discovered that the alleged molester had been away on a trip and only the friend and her mother were at home when the "touching of her privates" allegedly occurred.

Subtle Seductions

Most of us are aware of the great mental harm done to a youngster who is sexually molested by an adult. Not infrequently, the adult is the parent. Understandably these children find it most difficult to adjust to a normal life. If one cannot trust a parent, who can be trusted?

What is not so readily known is that there can be a more subtle form of seduction which can also inflict much harm on the developing mind of the child.

Often we smile as we talk about the five-year-old daughter who shows a preference for her father, or the five-year-old boy who prefers his mother and talks of marrying her. These feelings are quite normal and need not be discouraged. They are an important phase in the heterosexual development of the child. But when the child's preference for the parent of the opposite sex begins to involve too much physical closeness, then firm discouragement is necessary. Wrestling, lying in bed together, sitting too often and too long on a parent's lap, bathing an older child, parents walking about in the nude, are all situations which should be avoided. Often I have seen such situations encouraged by the parent. I am referring to a form of seduction often unconsciously pursued by one parent and so subtle as to escape the attention of the other parent. I can best illustrate this by describing some cases I have treated.

R. F. was an eleven-year-old girl who had bed-wetting as one of her problems. The father worked until late in the evening. On his return from work at about midnight he would literally carry his still sleepy daughter to the toilet, lower her pajamas, and when she was finished would dry her and return her to bed. Should she have wet herself before his arrival, he would then wash her body with a wash cloth, powder her and change her pajamas and the bedsheet. When I told him to discontinue this practice he looked at me as though I had a "dirty mind." I persisted in my suggestion. Within two weeks after he stopped this practice, the bed-wetting stopped.

Sometimes our suggestions are met with a stare that seems to say, "But, Doctor, how can you think of such a thing?" Then I am reminded of the story of the youngster who on being asked by a psychologist to describe what he saw, stated "penis" to a picture of a cylinder. A round object was described as a vagina. The psychologist then stated, "You appear to have sexual matters on your mind." To which the child replied, "You show me dirty pictures and then you say I have sex on my mind." Parents have often described situations which are sexually stimulating to the child only to turn about and accuse the doctor of looking at everything with sex on his mind.

On Nudity

The proponents of the idea of a child's growing up "free," so that he had no inhibitions have among them those who propose that children be exposed to nudity. Siblings and parents are told not to be embarrassed and to simply parade their unadorned bodies about in each other's presence. These people fail to recognize a simple truth. Children, all on their own, without any sort of pressure, develop a sense of modesty. And this modesty when it is shown should be respected and not belittled or laughed at.

I and many of my colleagues have seen children who on exposure to their parent's nude body were either sexually stimulated or in later years (here I rely on my experience with adults) had sexual difficulties. It is simply that the genitals of the parent become difficult to blot out, even though the child has become an adult looking at his or her marriage partner. And the thought of incest becomes most threatening.

Brotherly Hate

The difference between brotherly hate and brotherly love is that the former is instinctual and the latter is learned. Since instinct comes before learning, we're going to have to accept the fact that siblings will hate one another before they learn to love each other.

As a father of four, I can well appreciate how trying it is to drive a car or eat at a table when youngsters seem to be endlessly bickering, quarreling, and yelling. Where did it begin? How do we control it?

Love Is a Complex Thing

The rivalry so keenly felt by every child (it will vary in degree but it is universal) begins with his need for love by his parents. I mean love in its broadest sense—encompassing warmth, security, attention, acceptance.

When a child feels someone is endangering these most precious things, he will react with fear and hate. When we fully realize that the child is not bad or evil but feels threatened in some manner which he may not even understand, we are in a better position to do something constructive to control the degree of rivalry and hate. I say control because we can never fully eradicate it. And a little later I will show why we would not want to eradicate it because there is a very healthy side to it as well.

Rivalry, Bigamy, and Polygamy

What has rivalry to do with bigamy and polygamy? It can help illustrate to parents the feeling of rivalry that is felt by their children. How would a mother feel if her husband were to walk in one day and announce to her, "Helen, I should like you to meet Jane. She will be my second wife and will live with us and share our home and food. Since she is frightened and new here, I will have to spend more time with her and she will have to have more privileges than you. The bed we once slept in will now be shared by Jane and me." Helen would have good reason to be shocked. "What's wrong with me? Haven't I fully satisfied you? Why should you want another wife? Don't I matter any more? Do you still care what happens to me now, or are you more worried about Jane? Do you love Jane more than me?" These are the questions which are comparable to those asked and felt by a child when faced by the birth of a sibling. You can no more expect a wife to gladly accept a second woman in the home or a husband accept another man in the home.

Regression and Advancement

Their enormous need for love and attention causes many children to regress when a new child is brought home. Since the mother washes, powders, and changes the baby when he has a bowel movement, little Jimmy, age three, will unconsciously have a bowel movement to attract the mother's attention. Fortunately, it does not end there because this need for love and attention will also motivate the child to advance himself. The school-age child attempts to find love and acceptance outside the home as well. He wants to be accepted by the teacher, who is, after all, a substitute parent, and will do his utmost to please her. He will compete with his peers and attempt to excel. This is healthy. (Of course, like many good things, it should not be overdone.) It is the preschooler at home, and particularly if he is the first child, who carries the greatest burden of adjusting to a sibling rival.

Reassure, Reassure, Reassure, Reassure

Children require repeated reassurance of a parent's love and acceptance. They always seem to be so unsure of it—and for a good many reasons. Let us take this resentment towards their rival at home, for example.

As we saw above, Jimmy, age three, sees his mother paying extra attention to baby and in his mind the attention paid to the baby is equated with the mother's love for the baby. The baby has a bowel movement and mother has to hold the baby while she powders him and changes the diaper. So Jimmy, who is toilet trained, has a bowel movement, and somehow he doesn't get the same response from mother. She seems angry and most displeased at having to change Jimmy. "Surely she doesn't love and accept me any more," is Jimmy's feeling. "She loves the darned baby more. I hate it. Why doesn't she take that ugly thing back to the hospital? Who needs it?"

Let us move ahead a few years and realize that the pressures on the children have not let up. They are still acting as though they are unsure of just where they stand when it comes to their parents' love. Children, as we have seen, are unique. One might have a feature such as blue eyes or curly hair which endears him to a parent or grandparent. One seems brighter in some learning area. The child is astute enough to appreciate that he hasn't a quality or qualities which the parent desires (or worse—he has one which the parent detests), and he begins to wonder where he stands.

"All men are created equal. . . ." so says the Constitution of the United States. The fact remains that we are not all equal in looks or intelligence or in many other qualities. Yet we must constantly reassure each child that he is accepted for what he is—and mean it. When we can do that, we go a long way towards alleviating the pressure felt by a child because of the presence of a rival. It will also go a long way toward diminishing the intensity of brotherly hate.

Down the Stairs and into the Fire

Often it will seem that our efforts are failing. When our second son was born and our oldest was two years old, my wife tried having the two-year-old assist her with some simple chores, both to get the work done and to give her a chance to be with him and praise his efforts. The laundry was duly collected in the bedroom and put into a large bag which Barry delightedly helped throw down the stairs. He followed its descent with the words, "Now let's throw Daniel down."

I too made every effort to spend time with Barry. Daniel as an infant was content with his food and sleep and didn't need me so much. Barry and I built a fire. He was happy to help put some twigs into the fireplace. As the fire engulfed the twigs he calmly looked at me and said, "Now let's put Daniel in."

How can we perceive hate as having any element of health? We can when we realize that a child's hatred for his sibling rival can be a powerful force in his attempting to excel. In his attempt to keep what was felt to be a favored place, the number-one spot, the first-born often shows greater drive and motivation. Frequently they are at the top of the class and not infrequently go into the field of medicine. Some become surgeons and sublimate their aggression into healthy endeavor. They can cut and cure at the same time.

Unconscious Rivalry

It is not infrequent that in psychiatry we see a child or an adult who in his early years has begun to manifest ill behavior in his endeavor to hold onto the love and security of his parents which, for some reason, he felt was being lost. It can happen to a child no matter what his numerical position in the family. Several cases I have seen can illustrate some of the difficulties we sometimes encounter.

One youth of seventeen began to use addicting drugs. Interestingly, it was done in an unusual manner—the boy carefully studied and learned about each drug in a medical text before he used it. When we found that an older brother was diabetic and required daily injections of insulin, we began to understand what the younger brother was doing. An important, though by no means the only, reason the younger brother began to use drugs was his unconscious attempt to bring attention to himself. Concerned about the diabetic son's health, the parents were now forced to show equal concern for the younger brother and his use of drugs.

A young girl of fourteen I had been treating found herself involved with boys far beyond the degree we could consider normal, even in these liberal days. Rosalind dwelt upon the excitement she felt was generated at her home by talk of her sister's coming engagement to a suitor whom her mother was manipulating towards the altar. Her mother's expressed consent to the older daughter for an active sex role played no small part in Rosalind's developing promiscuity. Unconsciously Rosalind was still competing for mother's love. She was doing what the mother loved her sister for.

Divide and Conquer

There are times in family life when tensions are generated by too much "togetherness," and a little "apartness" proves beneficial. Each child is an individual, and not only enjoys but needs to spend some time alone with a parent. Although it might be difficult to arrange, devoting an hour or so completely to one child (such as a lunch at his favorite hamburger stand) can prove very rewarding to both parent and child. This is an opportunity to prove to an older child that although a new little one may receive a great deal of attention, an older child has other privileges in the family.

Most children look forward to a visit from a playmate, but it can sometimes turn into bedlam. Older siblings have a way of teasing or enticing away a younger brother or sister's guest, while little ones want to be part of the fun, and tend to tag along. It is not unusual for someone to end up crying, either because he is left out, or is not allowed to enjoy his friend alone. Mother comes in and suggests that "everyone play nicely together." She can't understand why the children themselves couldn't arrive at such a reasonable solution. The trouble is that it is not a reasonable solution. A child should have the privilege of having a friend of his own, without sharing or competing with others for his attention. The most feasible way to handle these conflicts is by attempting to avoid them. Inviting other children over when an older child is in school or a younger one is napping will prove more satisfying to everyone.

The Rival's Arrival

Preparing for the rival's debut is much easier when parents can understand the threat it poses to the older child. The greatest threat is to the first-born who is a preschooler and when the new arrival is the second-born.

The older child will question his new role. He may have heard that someone had bought a new car and traded in the old one. "Is this to happen to me?" the child may ask himself. It is important to have him feel that there is not to be any displacement. He will feel it anyhow. But we can help diminish the intensity of such a feeling. How? By keeping things as they had been as much as possible. This means not changing his sleeping quarters for one. If there are changes to be made, do them months before the new-born arrives. While mother is at the hospital it would be best if the child could remain at his own home with someone he knows well. Sending him to any strange environment will only add to his feelings of displacement. When the baby comes home do try to have gifts for the older child as well. One mother I know had simple packages of her child's favorite candies prepared. Whenever a well wisher arrived with a gift for the newborn, there was also the candy "left" for the older child. By appreciating the feelings of the older child and by simple thoughtful acts we can reassure the older child of our continuous love and his uninterrupted security.

Smotherly Love

As parents we are concerned that our children be properly nourished. If they are poorly fed they become malnourished and can succumb to such illnesses as scurvy, associated with a Vitamin C deficiency, or rickets, due to a lack of Vitamin D. On the other hand, if they are overfed they become obese and are prone to such illnesses as hardening of the arteries and diabetes. Sounds like a tightrope again, doesn't it? Well, the same is true with regard to emotional health. Too little love and security and the child suffers from emotional starvation. Too much overprotection—smotherly love, because it smothers as it possesses and protects—and we find our children having difficulties. Just as the overfed fat child cannot run well on the athletic field, so the overprotected child cannot perform well in the field of life.

We must, as parents, understand not only our child's needs but must look at our own needs and how at times they conflict with the needs of our children. We have seen how a child must learn to say, "Goodbye mama, goodbye papa." And we, as parents, must be able to say, "Goodbye, child." The child must be allowed to grow up to feel secure and independent, to have faith in his ability to stand alone. This important step of reaching into a difficult world cannot be accomplished unless the parent permits it.

The need for affection, of feeling wanted and belonging, is strong in all of us, children and parents alike. When there are difficulties in the relationship between parents, the object of such needs often is transferred to the child. Difficulties then arise for the child as well as the parent. The damage inflicted is often not seen until later years. As a psychiatrist who treats both children and adults, I have seen the difficulties of such a relationship during its formative stage and have treated adults in whom the damage had already taken place.

The Mater Martyr and Her Girl

Some mothers who tell themselves and their children and all who will listen how much they have sacrificed for their children have often made a sacrifice of their children for their own unconscious needs. Let us see how the mater martyr in pursuing her needs leaves behind a frustrated, confused and anxious child filled with the unresolved conflict of wanting love and desiring independence, but filled with the fear that in seeking independence one chances the loss of a parent's love.

W. C. was thirty-two when she consulted me. A comely woman, she had been married five years and had given up her teaching position to raise her daughter. Her present difficulty was marked anxiety, the onset of which occurred immediately upon learning of her mother's hospitalization with a stroke. During our first hour she informed me that she was an only child and had a very close relationship with her mother. In succeeding hours with me she spoke more about this relationship.

Her parents were proprietors of a small grocery store and worked many long hours. In her early years the family occupied a small apartment behind the store. Mrs. C. was not only a witness to the struggles of her parents in attempting to earn a livelihood, but was constantly reminded by her mother that they scrimped and saved so that she could eventually go to college and become a teacher. Go to college she did, and she finally received her teacher's license. And her mother continued to wear the same threadbare coat and to remind her daughter that such sacrifices enabled her to go to college. The daughter was both grateful and resentful. She was grateful that her parents did support her during her college days. But she resented the continual reminders and particularly the criticism her mother had of any boy she dated.

It seemed that no man was good enough for her mother's approval. She more than once stated that no man would sacrifice for her what her own mother did. Escape into marriage was most difficult. The normal desires of young adults finally presented both a problem and a solution. Even her mother agreed that marrying Irwin was superior to obtaining an illegal abortion. Mrs. C.'s mother did not enjoy the normal pleasures of becoming a grandmother. Sadly, she could only see herself cut out of her daughter's life and bitterly complained about the sad lot of mothers, who do so much for their children, only to have their children turn from them.

As parents, let us bear in mind the tale of the father who, on a journey with his son, comes upon a stream. Without hesitation the father lifts his son on his shoulders and wades across the stream. Lowering his son on the opposite shore, he asks, "When I am old and cannot swim, will you bear me across such streams on your shoulders?" His son replies, "I fear, Father, that by then I too shall have my son to carry."

Mrs. C.'s mother would not permit her daughter the normal joys of motherhood. Feelings of guilt were always left intermingled with expensive baby gifts. How Mrs. C. wished her mother would not trouble her and allow her to live happily with her husband and child! Unconsciously she wished that her mother did not exist. It was this wish that lay behind her feelings of panic when her mother was hospitalized. In treatment she began to accept her feeling of wanting to be rid of her mother. She began to realize that this desire was not responsible for her mother's being near death. The anxiety gradually diminished, her mother survived and recovered fairly well, reveling in the extra attention she received. As a result of treatment, Mrs. C. was able to resolve her conflicts about her mother. She was grateful for what treatment did and felt that her mother could also benefit from treatment. She had the social worker at the hospital recommend it only to have her mother exclaim, "Who, me? You must be crazy yourself to even think of such a thing."

Parents usually make sacrifices for their children. Whether it's a mother who takes on a job so as to save for her child's college education or a father who works hard to make ends meet, we are there to see that our children have the necessities of life and more. But when the mother who is doing her duty continually points out to her child how she has done without necessities for herself so that her child could have some luxury, she is implying that she and only she could be depended upon to care for the child. The child then finds himself smothered by a crippling conflict of a desire for and a fear of independence.

Papa's Girl

A smotherly kind of love need not be limited to mother and child. We see it often with father and child as well. It may be overlooked by many who see the relationship as one in which the daughter is "devoted." Nonsense. Too often that "gentle, devoted soul" is a frightened little child who may strike back in a neurotic way that is harmful to herself and her father too. Here again I can best illustrate this type of relationship by describing a young woman I have seen.

Peggy C. was a pretty, thirty-year-old woman who looked younger than her age. When she called to make the first appointment, she questioned whether in fact she needed psychiatric help. It was evident that she did, but she was primarily interested in her immediate difficulties at the time she called. Miss C. lived with her father in a small three-room apartment, the same apartment she once shared with both parents until the mother died of cancer ten years before. Why did an attractive, bright girl continue in an unmarried state and in these more liberal days continue to live with her father in a drab apartment in a run-down neighborhood? The answer lay in the relationship that had been established in her early childhood years. Mother and father were described as "always quarreling." "Whenever my father wanted something done, he asked me to do it. If it was getting his suit to the cleaners or ironing a shirt, it was me he turned to." In other words, the father behaved at times in such a manner as to have daughter act as his wife. When Mrs. C. became ill with breast cancer Peggy was sixteen. At her mother's death she was twenty and working as a secretary, and was by then the complete housekeeper at home. And so it continued during the years, father depending on Peggy and Peggy feeling guilty about leaving and also deriving some unconscious gratification from continuing the relationship. But things were beginning to fall apart—and badly. Miss C. had some years before begun an affair with a gambler, a man eighteen years her senior and married. A joint bank account Peggy had with her father was almost depleted of several thousands in savings. Not only was father beginning to ask about where the bank book was, but "Frankie" was pressuring her to embezzle company money so as to cover some bets he had made. He assured her he would get the money back to her "before the boss finds it missing." But his reassurances over the years were always promises that never seemed to materialize. Now she was frightened of father's wrath and the possible loss of her lover. Fortunately, and yet perhaps unfortunately, "Frankie" got his money elsewhere and she stopped being pressured by her father for the bank book, as he had changed his mind about some investment. She seemed relieved and at that point she decided to end her treatment, showing no desire to pursue a difficult course of therapy which required her effort in trying to understand some causes for her difficulties. She might have come to understand the neurotic relationship that existed between her parents, between herself and her parents, and how she attained some gratification as a child whose father favored her more than her mother, a situation that was carried into later years. I do not know what has since happened to Miss C. The chances are that life has not changed for her, a lonely and difficult life that is the direct outgrowth of a poor relationship between parents and the smothering love of a father.

Kids Get Hurt

We live in a world filled with pains and pleasures. Try as we may, we cannot possibly protect our children from all pains, whether physical or emotional—nor should we want to. Children must learn to live on their own, and they cannot if they do not learn to live with the pains that life has in store for every one of us—child and adult.

Needless to say, I do not advocate that we seek to have pain inflicted upon our children. But it is important that we accept ourselves as mortals whose legacy can be a child capable of caring for himself when we are no longer there to protect him. Here again it may seem like a tightrope. Yet there is solid middle ground where a child can feel protected and be taught to face difficulties that he is sure to encounter as he matures.

Harold G. was a ten-year-old boy who got a lot of protection but no lessons in self-reliance. I saw him and his parents in a consultation requested by his school principal. Harold was a handsome, freckle-faced boy, tall and well built for his age. He was an only child and, seeing him nestled between his parents on the sofa in my office, one got the feeling of a close-knit family unit. Just what the doctors call for—only too much so. Anyway, too close between mother and son. Harold's difficulties were clearly visible to his classmates and teacher, but not to his mother. He was described as an anxious child who was visibly fearful of participating in any sports at school, was immaculately attired at the end as well as the beginning of the day, clung to his teachers, and was, despite his size, the butt of jokes by his peers with such comments as "fag" and "mama's boy" blurted in his direction. Mother's description of Harold's classmates was that they were "horrible examples of the products of a decaying moral culture." Quite a mouthful! A session with her alone revealed a most anxious woman, fearful of hurt or loss of her son, "my most prized possession." After six barren years, visits to sterility specialists, nights filled with thermometer and temperature chart, sex without joy but only with the thought of conception, she had finally had Harold. Little wonder that he meant so much to her. But Mrs. G. had to learn to let go. Boys do play ball and, yes, some do get hurt doing so, but certainly not to the degree that we don't want our children to participate. Yes, some boys do get hurt riding bicycles, but with proper safety measures taken, boys of ten should be allowed to use their bicycles to go to school, traffic and weather permitting. True, children do get colds in rainy weather—but in a slight drizzle should mother be standing there in the school hall with umbrella and boots? These were some of the specific subjects Mrs. G. brought up when asked whether some of her son's difficulties might be due to her overprotecting him, Fortunately, she was capable of understanding how her own fears were interfering with her son's proper emotional development. Progress towards removing the "s" from "smotherly love" was being made when she was able to talk about her role in Harold's refusal to go to camp, his finally going with a cousin, and her bringing him home a week later. She again had some unkind words—for his counselor. Seeing mother and son for some months had beneficial results for both. Harold found it easier to separate from his mother, could now tolerate the give and take of boys his age at camp and at school, and mother was more able to see that the safety of the nest she made for him offered no safety after all.

Send My Boy Home

I wish I had also been able to help Mr. L. W., who, although thirty-four, presented the same problems, only twenty-four years later. An only child, he saw me because of severe anxiety associated with moving to his own apartment. For many years he slept in a cot in the living room of his mother's apartment, although financially able to maintain his own quarters. His mother called, insisting that I tell him that he ought to move back to her, or surely he would suffer a nervous breakdown. I feel I made an error in indicating to her that her son was my patient and that I was primarily interested in his getting well and not interested in her feelings that her son return to her. Had I veered from the classical approach of dealing with him alone and brought mother into treatment as well, I might have succeeded. Perhaps. In any event, she prevailed upon him to leave treatment with me.

Father Knows Best?

Sometimes a father by word and deed blocks the normal independent striving of his son's future plans. How many of us are witnesses to a father's protest of how he has slaved to build up a business only to have his son spurn it? Or the doctor or lawyer who shows his keen disappointment because his son has other aspirations? I can cite numerous instances of how a father's pressures for a son to aspire in the father's chosen direction led to misery for both father and son. If a son desires to follow in his father's footsteps, that is perfectly all right. But pressure which seems to say that unless he does he loses father's love and probably will perish on his own can only lead to disaster for all concerned.

Semper Fidelis

While on duty in the navy, I was assigned the task of helping one of the cadets who was enrolled in a preparatory program for the naval academy. Robert W. was a handsome six-footer with an I.Q. of 138. Bright and capable, he could have been an asset to any school. Yet he was having difficulty in completing his assignments, refused to follow simple regulations, and in general was a source of irritation to his teachers and officers.

I arranged an interview for him. Sitting erect, white cap in hands, he readily informed me of the cause of his difficulties in one sentence.

"Sir, I hate the navy."

"Then why are you in this voluntary program?"

"Sir, my father wants me to go to Annapolis just as he did and just as his father did before him. I don't, but he insists that I do."

He went on to talk of his desire to be an architect, of his wishing to marry his girl friend and of his hatred for the military. He associated the service with deprivation because as a child his father served (quite heroically) for years away from home in World War II. Robert's mind was quite fixed on the idea that he and his mother had suffered enough and that his future wife and child were not going to be deprived as he had been—whether in war or peace.

It was only two more weeks before graduation from his preparatory program and Robert was becoming more restless. Before plans could be made for an interview with his father, Robert saw to it that the marines were to come to his rescue in a most indirect way. On the weekend before graduation, Robert, who did not drink, somehow got roaring drunk and proceeded to smash up a civilian bar—it took several members of the U.S. Marine Corps to cart him off to the brig. He was still in the brig when his father met with me. A distinguished-looking, greying, erect naval captain, he was an older version of his son. I was pleased that he did not view me as a junior officer, but rather as a physician who was there to assist him and his son. He was hurt and shaken by the recent and explosive episode. What was wrong with his son? Sitting there together, I felt much sympathy for this bright, warm man who had fought bravely and now was suffering more mental anguish than during those bleak days in the cold Atlantic waters. Those dark nights were filled with fantasies of his coming home to see his son grow into manhood—and attend the academy. And now this.

It came as a surprise to him when I told him that his son held the navy responsible for the years of deprivation he felt while his father was away. Following several hours of discussion the father began to understand how his own desires were in direct conflict with his son's. He agreed that unless he allowed his son to resign from the program, the form of behavior we were witnessing would only continue. A difficult decision, but a wise one.

Kids Get Sick

Any illness, whether of a child or an adult, always has an emotional component. When a child is sick, he has feelings about his illness, and we parents also have feelings about our children being sick. The child may feel sad or guilty or perhaps even glad. And we parents also have a multitude of feelings, perhaps guilt or sadness or anger or, most likely, a mixture of all these feelings.

Let us take a closer look at some of these feelings and how the unconscious may be playing a significant role in physical illnesses. When we can understand the emotional part of the illness—the child's as well as ours—we are in a much better position to do something constructive for the child's mental health.

The Pleasure of His Pain

Robert H. was twenty-five when he was referred to me by his family physician. For several months he had been thoroughly checked by his family doctor, and had had numerous tests for his abdominal distress. Nothing could be found to cause his complaints and the doctor suggested that there might be an emotional causative factor which ought to be discussed with a psychiatrist. Mr. H. had his doubts but was willing to talk things over. In our first interview I learned that he had been married for two years and had a daughter aged six months. On learning this last fact I remembered that his complaints coincided with the birth of his daughter. He easily spoke of his work in the field of law, his colleagues, his parents, his younger sister. His major concern was his stomach pains and he was beginning to worry about his colleagues and

superiors at work, who made it known to him that he was
letting his work slip and remained at home too much. At the
end of our first session I suggested that we meet again. He
questioned the need of seeing a psychiatrist for what he felt
was mere physical distress. I could only point out to him that
all other avenues of approach to his problem had been taken
and it might prove beneficial to continue. Reluctantly, he
agreed.

We met for many more sessions, sometimes after a day of
his remaining at home because of his "pains." One day his
wife called to say, "I've had it." Although he was in treatment, the pains seemed to be getting worse. I informed Mr.
H. of his wife's call and with his permission I invited Mrs. H.
to join us for a session. In his presence she described him as "a
whining little child" not unlike their little girl, and "much
more." "It's like catering to two children." Following that
session Mr. H. spoke a little more freely of his demands at
home, something he was reluctant to discuss until his wife so
forcefully described them. Although at an earlier session he
could not remember being ill as a child, he now began to
recall his remaining at home quite frequently during his first
years at school. If it wasn't an earache, it was a sore throat or
a stomach ache. He recalled at one session, with an almost
obvious sigh of pleasure, how his mother would put him to
bed, read to him and cater to his every wish when he was ill.
A stomach ache was good for at least two days of catering. I
pointed out to him the pleasure he seemed to derive from his
being ill. "But that was then," he quickly replied. "And now,
too," I responded. Slowly the pieces of the jigsaw puzzle that
our lives are made of began to fit together. Mr. H. began to
recall feelings of sibling rivalry. And when we consider the
fact that he was just five years older than his sister, we can
begin to understand his unconsciously using illness as a means
of remaining home when he began school and his little rival
had their mother all to herself. It was quite difficult for an
intelligent, sophisticated young man to think of himself as
repeating in later years a pattern of behavior he established
two decades ago. And very difficult to see himself as looking
upon his own child as a rival for his wife's attention and love.
Happily, Mr. H. began to see his residual childish needs, was

able to "let go," and has been free of symptoms for some time.

The above illustrates something all parents should be aware of—the often unconscious pleasurable factor of being ill and being taken care of. Do not for a moment think I am advocating that we do not show concern and do whatever is proper for our sick children. But do be aware of how a child may unconsciously, and at times consciously (such as on exam day) use illness as an excuse. It is then that we must be firm and not coddle the child. If there are problems, an attempt must be made to have them brought out in the open and dealt with. Sometimes this requires professional help as seen in the next case I should like to discuss.

Never on Weekends

Elsa was seven when she began to complain of severe headaches. She was seen by her pediatrician, who could find no cause and recommended an ophthalmological examination. Her eyes were found to be normal. Elsa continued to complain of severe frontal headaches sometimes lasting for hours.

She was again seen by the pediatrician and this time her mother brought up another matter that was troubling the parents. Elsa had always done well academically and that week a report card indicated a marked underachievement. Mother also confessed that Elsa seemed cranky and demanding. All associated with the headaches? Just the normal ups and downs of a seven year old? There were many unanswered questions in the pediatrician's mind.

Although quite busy, he took the time out to explore what he began to suspect—some emotional difficulties. By his astute questioning he learned a fact the mother never brought to his attention. Elsa started having her difficulties when her mother returned to teaching. When were the headaches most severe? When did they occur? The last question, when answered completely, was a most important clue. By fixing specific dates, it was found that they never occurred on weekends!—an excellent piece of detective work that made my job much easier when I was asked to see Elsa.

When I am asked to see a child on consultation, I like to see the entire family together for the first session. You would be amazed as to how much can be learned by seeing them all together—even where each member of the family chooses to sit can be informative. The three of them sat down on a sofa, Elsa between her father and mother. It gave us all an opportunity to discuss the reasons for our meeting. Mother did most of the talking and discussed essentially all of the above. Elsa seemed puzzled, as any seven-year-old might, that she had headaches and all that was being done is that we were talking about them. It is not an easy task for an adult to consider that a physical ailment may be caused by some unconscious factors. It is much more difficult for the child.

I next saw each of them individually. The mother was a pleasantly attractive woman of thirty. She spoke at length about her work. She had taught at elementary school a little more than two years before the birth of Elsa and now was again teaching—only this time, after some more training, she was teaching a small class of organically brain-injured children. She spoke of feeling very good at doing a difficult and specialized teaching job. We spoke of her family; she was the only girl in a family of four; all three brothers were professionals. We spoke of her life with her husband. No difficulties—oh, yes, just one, mentioned almost casually. They wished they could have had at least one more child. Pursuing this, it became apparent that this was a most painful subject for her. There would be time to pursue it further at some later date.

Elsa's father was a tall, thin man who managed a store. He spoke of feeling somewhat guilty about not finishing college but felt he was doing well in his field and was soon to be promoted. He seemed content with life. When asked about a desire for more children, he stated that he was aware of his wife's feeling quite depressed about it. They had seen medical specialists who could find nothing wrong with either parent. He readily accepted the status quo.

Little Elsa was a delight to work with. She came for our interview literally skipping into the room. She seemed happy to talk to someone and spoke of her headache that morning as her mother was preparing her breakfast before leaving for her job some forty minutes away. Elsa was very able to describe her feelings of loneliness when eating her breakfast by herself (her father left quite early). No, she wasn't aware of any reason why she was doing poorly at school.

I arranged for further meetings with her mother. What clearly developed was mother's need to understand her own sense of lack of fulfillment and feeling of inadequacy resulting from her feeling of inability to bear another child. Also her continued feeling of rivalry with her brothers. Her special job gave her the status she so desired. And Elsa began to understand that she felt her mother's interest in her job as a rival and her headaches as an attempt to have her remain home with her—hence headaches, but never on weekends. It was no coincidence that Elsa had headaches and the mother was interested in children with "brain damage."

Treatment for both had a desired beneficial result. The headaches disappeared, school work was up to par, and the mother began to accept herself as an adequate woman, which she was.

We can from this case learn that a child's physical complaints may have their roots in feelings which they can't quite comprehend. A child like Elsa may feel the same rivalry with her mother's job as she would with a new child. And we can see that often the stresses of a parent, though unconscious, can set in motion a reaction in the child which compounds the difficulty.

Don't Kid Kids

We are often tempted to avoid the truth when dealing with our children. We sometimes lie and make a difficult situation more difficult. Or we try to reassure a child in pain by telling him it doesn't hurt or that it will not hurt when we want his cooperation. Simply stated, one should not kid kids. The truth is far less painful to child and parent.

When I was eight I had a small mole on my forehead. My mother was concerned and took me to the family doctor. I looked forward to going there because I liked sitting in his huge (I was smaller then) leather chair in the waiting room, and he let me look into his microscope. To me he was godlike and could do no wrong. But that day he did, and I still can't forget it. He looked at the mole, said it wasn't anything to be concerned about and could easily be removed. Years later I still recall his going for a cotton applicator that he dipped into a bottle, all the time assuring me that it wouldn't hurt. What a lie! It was a most searing pain because it was acid that he used. It hurt—but the pain of his not telling the truth was somehow more painful.

When a child is ill or in pain don't say it doesn't hurt. You can sympathize, and do what you can to reassure the child, all without pampering.

When a child has to see the doctor or go to the dentist or even a child psychiatrist, do tell him what you are going for. Children are very able to accept the truth and cooperate in their own behalf. On several occasions, after asking a child in his parents' presence why they were coming to see me, I was told such things as "I don't know, I was told I was going for a toy." This, after I informed the parents they were to be truthful with their child! The parents' explanation was that they feared the child would protest and not come. A parent can be firm in asking a child to do what is in the child's best interest. Tell the truth and the child develops the trust and confidence that is essential in his relationship with you.

I know it often appears quite difficult to be honest with a child when we want his cooperation in taking unpleasant medicine, for example. I recall when I tended to one of my sons when he was about two years old and had a gastrointestinal illness. I tried having him take some not-too-pleasant-tasting medication but he kept pointing to his abdomen and saying it was his tummy that hurt and I should put the medicine on it.

Telling the child that the medicine might not taste good but is important in his getting well is the correct thing to do. Saying it tastes delicious when it doesn't will surely lose his respect for your words and make it far more difficult for him to take further medications.

The Doctor's Doctor

In choosing a dentist or pediatrician for my children I not only look for competence in his field, but for an individual who can be honest with my child, sympathize with him when he has to, and give him his shots or drill his teeth when necessary without frightening him or lying to him. Explaining to the child how and why something is done can have a calming effect. It will take more of the professional's time, but it is necessary and beneficial.

One of my children was ready to bolt out of the dentist's waiting room the first time he was there. He was called in and some of the simple instruments that were to be used (such as the little mirror) were explained to him. He sat quietly throughout the examination, interested in all that was being explained. A firm yet reassuring tone does far more good than a threatening gesture by either the professional or the parent.

Our children accept the doctor's word when he says, "This doesn't hurt," because he will also warn them when something is going to hurt.

Desertion at the Hospital

Here I should like to tell you how to prepare your child emotionally for his being abandoned at the hospital. It would be unnecessary if only hospital administrators could feel as threatened as does the child when left in some room or ward instead of being able to have his parents there. Some hospital administrators are well aware of a child's emotional needs and do make arrangements for the parent to sleep near the child. But most hospitals are still sadly archaic about this.

Here again, whatever the reason or the procedure, the doctor and parent should hopefully take the time to explain to the child the reasons for hospitalization. The only time a child can accept doubt and ignorance about why and when he is going to the hospital is when he is in a coma.

Parents Get Sick

The *I* in Ch*I*ld

It will help us to understand why it is important that
children be told the truth by our discussing the *I* in ch*I*ld. To
a child's way of thinking, everything revolves around him. It is
all *I*, rarely he or she or they. So if something happens, it is
also *I*. If a parent has an accident or becomes ill, the child
somehow feels involved or responsible—the *I* is there. Name
any distressful situation—death, divorce, illness, and the child
questions his role in what is happening and may feel responsible and guilty. To prevent or alleviate such feelings it is
essential that we be honest with the child and tell as much as
can be understood by the particular child at his age.

Go Away, I Don't Need You

Parents, particularly mothers who have been hospitalized or
have been away for several days or longer, are often shocked
by the greeting of their young ones left behind. It is a greeting
that seems to say, "Go away, I don't need you."

When our second son was born, our eldest, Barry, was two
years old. I remember holding Daniel, the infant, as my wife,
on returning from the hospital entered the door and rushed
toward Barry to embrace him. Struggling out of the embrace,
Barry muttered, "Go away!"—a shocking greeting to his mother, who stood there with tears in her eyes. Yet this is the
greeting that normally occurs as the child attempts to protect
himself against feelings of abandonment by trying to tell
himself that the individual so essential for security really isn't
necessary.

It is desirable for parents to be aware of such feelings and not to respond with harshness and disapproval. It is merely a child's mind trying to protect himself. Within days this need of rejecting the alleged rejector (who went away) is gradually overcome, and the child is nestling next to the mother, wanting her very much and again fearful of abandonment.

Witness to a Trauma

There is a vast difference between informing a child honestly and sympathetically about some illness of his parent and the child's being a witness to the traumatic event. Depending upon the age of the child and the circumstances, certain traumatic experiences can have a lasting bad effect on the child, and he should be shielded from them.

A chronically ill and dying parent or sibling or other close relative should not be seen by children. Normally a dying individual should be in a hospital. If for any reason this is not possible, then all efforts should be made to have young children or even older children away so as to not be witness to an event that is much too traumatic for the child's mind to cope with healthily.

The strange and bizarre behavior of a mentally ill parent should also be kept from children. Again hospitalization is in order, but if this is not done having the child at another home can be helpful.

So often we may be so concerned with the ill person that we may tend to overlook the child and his needs. A situation like this involved a youngster of eight. His relatively young father had been found to have a birth defect involving the heart. Surgery was recommended to alleviate the condition. All was going well. The father had been hospitalized, had his open heart surgery and was recuperating at home. It was a difficult time for the young family and they were just beginning to feel a sign of relief when Timothy began having his difficulties. Nightmares, fear of exertion, talk of bad hearts and death were the major symptoms when Timothy was seen in consultation at a clinic. What developed was a picture of Timothy overexposed to a discussion of congenital heart defects (i.e. birth defects) which made him wonder about his own heart. He saw doctors come and go. Once a cylinder of oxygen and an oxygen tent were delivered to the house. All quite precautionary at the time, but in Timothy's eyes they were instruments for the doomed—him and his father.

Timothy needed a great deal of reassurance. It had to be explained that a parent's being born with a heart defect didn't mean he had one too. Timothy's problems were so directly related to the trauma he experienced that the unconscious factors (i.e. anger at father) were not dealt with. Timothy quickly responded to reassurance and such measures as using a stethoscope so he could hear his heart beat as well as the doctor's did much to alleviate the distress that resulted from an overexposure to trauma and too little explanation at home.

A Child Is but a Child

We often find well-meaning parents and relatives who attempt to calm a child when a parent is ill or hospitalized with such comments as, "You're the man now" or "You're the mother now." The child's mind cannot accept such a concept. In fact, such statements are extremely threatening to the child and should never be used.

Here again we have to take into consideration how the child's mind functions. For example, often the boy might wish that he were the man and would not have to acquiesce to father's demands. Suddenly he finds his father is ill and someone is telling him, "You're the man around the house." To the child it has but one meaning—his wish has come true and he was responsible for father's illness! Again let us realize that to the child it is always *I;* whatever happens somehow he is involved.

A Hospital Is Not a Resort

Some parents try to spare their child the pain of having him know that a parent is in the hospital. Often they will say that the ill parent went away on vacation. Somehow the child learns that the parent is not at a resort and is at a hospital. Inquiring neighbors, the distress on other family member's faces, all tend to frighten the child more than if he were told a more truthful story. One can explain a situation in terms that can be understood by the child and then one can reassure the youngster. But if an adult continues to hide behind a wall of lies, the child is sure to question what is going on. Ignorance and doubt can be very frightening to the child. He will worry about why they don't tell him the truth and begin to wonder more about what his role was in his parent's illness.

Kids Have Fears

Benjamin Franklin erred when he stated that life's certainties are death and taxes. He left out fears. We adults have our fears such as illness or death (or tax time). Our children also have their share of fears, many being of a transient nature during various developmental stages. A child's fears, such as of the dark, may come and disappear, only to emerge again without any seeming reason. Or the parents are surprised to see a child who never experienced fear of water suddenly become terrified of going into the water. Often we see no external cause for many of the fears children develop. Fortunately these fears come and go, like sore throats, earaches, and colds. We must learn to live with and accept them, as part and parcel of raising any child.

The Outside World Is Scary

As the child matures, his senses are all bombarded by thousands of sights and sounds. Some of them are quite scary at first. As a helpless little creature his mind and body must first learn to adjust to the many sounds and sights that will at first overwhelm him.

The toddler, as he explores his new-found world, will normally show many fears. He will cry at the turning on of a vacuum cleaner, frightened by the sound of its whirring motor. His ears are not yet attuned to the scary world of lightning and thunder, of roaring trains and speeding jets, of flushing toilets and jangling fire engine bells. His eyes and mind have yet to adjust to large overwhelming objects which seem so able to engulf and destroy him. His mind has yet to learn that a disappearing mommy does come back.

As he grows, new objects are to be feared—wild animals which may eat him, bad ghosts or boogie men who can attack him, other children who can hurt him, water in which he may drown, doctors who inject you, dentists who drill you, teachers who criticize you, friends who laugh at you, parents who don't understand you. I could go on and on. Suffice it to say there are many sights and sounds and situations which frighten children. Most are temporary and harmless. What do we do when they occur?

The Dos and Don'ts of Fears

Do accept the normalcy of children's fears. *Don't* regard them as something abnormal which must hurriedly be gotten rid of.

Do allow the child a period of adjustment. *Don't*, repeat, don't make fun of or shame him.

Do show him you can understand that having a fear is a legitimate difficulty of growing up. *Don't* force him into acts which can intensify the fear.

Let us examine the latter *don't* at greater length. Some parents feel as threatened when their child shows some fear as when he sucks his thumb or has some other habit about which the parent feels ashamed. The parents may feel that it is a reflection of their poor parenthood and worry that others may see that there is something wrong. The simple truth is that children do have fears and they are nothing to be ashamed of. Fears of children should not threaten parents into acts which can only intensify the child's difficulty. How many of us have been witness to a father throwing a frightened child into the water he dreads? Yes, some children have quickly gotten over their fear of water in such a manner, but what of the others who would never go swimming again? Who is willing to make a judgment as to how any fearful child is going to react? I know I won't. Better to allow a child the time he seeks in overcoming such a fear.

I'm Not Going to School

There is a fear which requires a modified version of what I suggest above—the school phobia. Some children, for various reasons, years after beginning school will develop a fear of going off to school. It may be related to leaving mother after the birth of a sibling, it may be fear of a teacher or reciting in class. Often the child is not really capable of knowing just why he does not want to go to school. If the reason is known, efforts can be made in the direction of remedying the cause. If the cause is not known it is safe to insist that the child go off to school. Take him if you have to. Be sympathetic and also firm. There have been instances in which a frantic parent has called me to tell me that his child has waked up and stated that he will not go to school. The exact reason cannot be determined. Without hesitation I recommend that the parent insist the child go. In most cases the parent would call a week or even months later to tell me all was well. Where the child is too large to haul and refuses to budge or where the fear of school is just one of a host of many difficulties, then professional help becomes necessary.

Fear of Failure

I was asked to see a youth of fourteen who suddenly developed a fear of going to school. In many cases, the difficulty is usually seen at an earlier age. Briefly, Sidney's difficulties began with his being transferred from a school in the city to a school in the suburbs. A serious, studious youth with an all-A average in the city schools, he suddenly found himself in the midst of a large number of similarly bright and studious youths where competing for A's became a formidable task. Instead of all A's, his first report showed a sprinkling of C's amongst some B's and A's. When I saw the school psychologist, I was informed that Sidney was having the same difficulties often seen in other youths who transferred from city schools. Fear of failure, of concomitant rejection and loss of love, was a prominent factor in his refusal to go to school. Able to face his fears when he discussed them in their true perspective, Sidney shortly returned to school.

In homes where there is too great an emphasis on performance, the fear of failure—and hence rejection—is often a powerful factor in a child's doing poorly in his academic work. The child becomes so crippled with conflicts that he withdraws from the threatening situation—his studies.

One youth I have seen with academic underachievement spoke candidly of his father, whom he admired, hated, and feared. "No matter how well I do, he always did better. Once I thought I had him. I got all A's. He looked at the report and said, 'That's what I expect.' Never an encouraging word, never a compliment, only criticism. That's when I gave up." Sounds out of the ordinary? From where I sit I see it so often I've begun to feel there is too much criticism and not enough acceptance and compliments.

Teachers can be guilty as well. Yesterday at a clinic where I see children for brief therapy, a boy of ten had tears in his eyes as he repeated what happened when he told his teacher he was to be absent in the afternoon so he could see me. "She turned to the class and said, 'Let's clap. George won't be here this afternoon.'" And this is a boy with slight brain damage whom we were trying to help! No doubt he was more difficult to teach, but certainly comments such as hers would only compound his difficulties—perhaps a fear of school as he becomes unable to handle his anger. This brings us to . . .

The Inner World Is Frightening

If the outside world is scary, the "inner world" is even more frightening because we can't see it, smell it, taste it, nor hear it. It is unconscious and we can only feel its discomfort. I am referring to the unconscious conflicts which manifest themselves through the individual child's irrational fears.

In our discussions of brotherly hate, we saw how the birth of a rivel set in motion feelings in a child which can at times frighten him. Life for all is filled with feelings which require compromise. We may feel hatred for a rival but we must not kill him. We may have intense sexual feelings but society demands that they be fulfilled in a certain manner. Because the child learns that certain feelings are wrong—or is so overwhelmed with fear of such feelings—the mind may seek escape from its true feelings to protect itself. For example, in a classic case of Freud's, a boy had an intense fear of horses. In analysis it developed that the child feared his father and the horse was only a symbol.

That is why we often speak of "irrational fears." There does not seem to be a logical reason for someone to have intense fear of a horse, for example, or of walking into a store. What has happened is that the feared object has had a symbol substituted for it.

A boy of thirteen I have seen suddenly feared walking into most stores. As the story developed, what he really feared was possible loss of control of his sexual urges. Stores with only men and elderly people were no threat. But stores with young salesgirls were threatening to him. The youth had to first learn what he unconsciously feared before he could cope with his problem.

Where there is an irrational fear, we are often dealing with a fear of loss of control. The two main areas where loss of control is feared are aggression and sexual feelings or a combination of the two.

Children not only see their brother and sister as rivals for their parents' love, they also feel a parent as a rival as well. It is natural for boys to feel an affinity for their mothers. But in so doing they may develop an intense fear of the large powerful father. Or a girl in preferring her father may begin to fear her mother (or a substitute for her).

Happily the situation most often does not end there; children learn to adjust into accepting what can and cannot be done.

Contagious Fears

We speak of people "catching colds" from one another. The same can be said of fears. When a child is exposed to adults with fears, often these fears are transmitted to the child. A simple example would be of a parent who fears riding in an airplane. The airplane as a feared object may be but a symbol for the parent (i.e. loss of control), but to the child it can represent a logical threat when it is seen as a dangerous means of transportation. By now you may be thinking, "Why does the airplane have to be a symbol to the parent for loss of control? It is a real danger." The fact is that in helping people with fears we often find that what is so "real" at first sight is not so real when we begin to see the unconscious conflicts of the mind.

The No-Help Help

I have had some personal experiences of how our help has been of no help when it came to fears of my children. I'm sure what we experienced has occurred to many others and we ought to be aware of it.

Children are often quite trying, particularly when they are quarreling among themselves. To quiet them, maids and baby sitters, I have found, will often threaten them. Once one of my children awoke with a nightmare. He described being in a crate and shipped overseas. The other children were also up by then and told us how a maid, with all good intentions, would admonish them and tell them that if they were bad they would when asleep be put in a box by the mailman and shipped away.

Often threats are made without our knowledge. It might be wise to tell all help that they are to make no threats of any sort to children. Too often instead of threatening them with loss of their favorite dessert, they will use ghosts, boogie men, and police who "will come." Once I was startled to see my younger children quite frightened on seeing a policeman near our hotel room while on a vacation. Our older son informed me that the baby sitter the night before told them they had better behave and go to bed or the police would come and punish them.

Discipline and Communication

Three-year-old Johnnie, who had been toilet trained, has a baby sister brought home and he soils himself. Mother slaps him. What do both acts have in common? Both are forms of communication. The difficulty is that neither John nor mother knew what the other was saying. In other words, communication can be by deeds (non-verbal) as well as by words (verbal).

When we consider discipline we must consider communication because all forms of discipline are forms of communication. Discipline is briefly defined as: 1—training; 2—controlling; 3—punishing.

If a parent asks, "Should I spank my three-year-old child for running across the street unattended?" he is really asking "Is spanking under the circumstances a proper form of communication?" or "If I spank my child, will he understand what I am trying to have him learn—that it is dangerous to cross the street at his age without me there?"

There are healthy forms of communication and unhealthy types.

First: To Understand

How do we properly communicate for a child's best emotional development? The answer first lies in understanding ourselves and our children. It is essential for proper communication that there be understanding.

If Johnnie's mother could have understood why Johnnie defecated in his pants after being toilet trained, then she could have been in the position to communicate feelings which would comfort him in his feelings of terror regarding his new rival. We can then begin to see that hitting him is not proper communication under these circumstances. It only reinforces his fear that he is being replaced and is not liked any more.

Granted there are times when any parent can feel, "I've had it" and might think, "To hell with understanding." Even then the act which follows, such as hitting the child, need not be disastrous. In a non-verbal way he can be telling the child that a parent also has limitations.

But it is sheer nonsense to go along with those who believe that modern parents are too concerned with proper psychological upbringing and all that is necessary is the old woodshed and a few good whacks on the child's behind. If we could get to understand ourselves better, to understand our needs, and get to understand what is normal and what is not for a child and what a child's needs are, then we are in a much better position to communicate with our children. I might add that what is true within the family unit could well be applied among groups of people and among nations. What is sorely lacking at all levels of communication is the understanding required for healthy communication to prosper.

The most vital element for the child's mental development is that there be proper communication with the people around him. Proper communication can prevent much grief in the child and his parents. It could certainly end bloodshed among nations.

Since all forms of discipline are forms of communication, the important question is the differences between good communication and poor communication. To repeat, good communication requires that the parent understand himself and understand his child. Understanding children is difficult, to be sure, but certainly not impossible. It would be a boon for future children if courses in normal child development were made part of the high school and college curriculum. Where do we start? Perhaps by experts in child development teaching future teachers who can then instruct future parents. Some readers would be amazed at the simple questions some parents will ask regarding their children. If we can even partially remove the cloak of ignorance that prevails regarding child development, we will go a long way in properly communicating with our children.

Often the normal act of a child is met with some form of punishment by his parents. We want our children to grow up mentally healthy, but you cannot expect normalcy if you communicate to your child that he is to be punished for some normal act.

If there were understanding of oneself and one's children, would the following form of communication be used? On careful reflection we will agree that the answer would be no.

Hit and Run

The Hit and Run phenomenon is one that leads to emotional starvation for the child. It is when a parent's (usually the father) communication seems limited to the end of a newspaper or the palm of the hand. It occurs when the father is chronically too enmeshed in his own pursuits to participate in active communication with the members of the family. You can picture him reading his paper or trade journal and the child doing something which he finds annoying. Silently rising out of his chair and wham! with the paper—then silently slinking back into his chair as though he had gotten the message across that there be peace and quiet when he is reading. The child, who was probably participating in an activity quite normal for his age, is puzzled. He has received a message but does not know what it really means. The child could well wish that his parent had learned to use his tongue as well as his eyes and hands.

Is Hitting Necessary?

The old adage of, "Spare the rod and spoil the child" is wrong. It should be, "Spare the communication and spoil the child."

But what about the boy of seven who pleaded with his father to hit him, or the terror of the third grade class who became angelic after having been given a good swat in his rear by his teacher? Am I advocating corporal punishment? No. I do not believe in hitting any child. Many parents do what was done unto them. I was never hit and I don't hit. But that is not the important point. The important thing that occurred with the children above is that rather than endure the agony of silence, they preferred communication—even if that communication was at the end of a hand or newspaper. Hit and run is bad communication, but no communication (i.e. silence) is the worst punishment of all.

Hit Me! Hit Me!

When Robert was an infant his father was still attending college. Then it was graduate school. Financial pressures, the normal wailing of an infant, the demands of examinations were all very trying. It was a difficult life for everyone. Unplanned and unwanted, Robert was sort of lost in the shuffle. By the time he was six and father was towards the end of his training, the birth of another child compounded the difficulties for the parents and Robert. He refused to go to school and tormented the infant whenever his mother's back was turned.

When the parents sought psychiatric help, Robert's father was candid in telling how he often found himself quite frustrated and would take Robert across his knees and "give him a few good slaps." He was advised to cease such hittings. What followed could at first seem puzzling until we realize how a child so desperately needs communication. When Robert's father began to handle his anger by ignoring his son, it frightened Robert even more. So upset did Robert become by his father's sullen silence that one day he pleaded with his father, "Hit me! Hit me!"

The Agony of Silence

Silence is agonizing loneliness for the child. Rather than endure the pains of abandonment he will seek punishment, because punishment brings with it a message that someone is there and does care. It may be a sick kind of communication, but it is more desirable than the agony of silence.

Acts of violence by abandoned children in the slums—or

elsewhere—are not only a manifestation of anger. There is a desire for punishment because punishment brings an authority figure. The child is no longer alone. Someone is forced to pay attention—to communicate—even if it is "The Man," that often maligned poor substitute for the real father. It is sad that anti-social acts become the method by which some abandoned children communicate with the hostile world. The difficulties are compounded and the vicious cycle goes round and round when society's communication is one of incarceration—again silence and abandonment.

Starvation in the Suburbs

People are people whether they live in the slums of the city or in some exclusive suburb. The problems of the children and their parents do not differ greatly from area to area. But the manner in which these problems manifest themselves may vary because of a particular environment. Let's take a look at some of the difficulties of the suburban child.

The Sometimes Father

A sometimes father can be found anywhere. But the sometimes father of the suburb is a distinct entity. He is the man who is sometimes home but often is not there when the child is awake. Chasing the almighty dollar to pay for the mortgage, the second car, a better vacation, he is often working later hours, always finding another business venture or improving the business he is in. It seems he is always working day and night towards a goal of greater economic security. Only he turns around and sees that he seems to have just as far to go year after year. The wife complains, but he answers, "What does she know about earning a living?" The children suffer not only because of his absence but often they become the target of mother's pent-up frustration and anger.

A Matter of Commitment

It is true that many a child has grown up emotionally healthy with a father who busied himself at work for long hours. Only a generation ago it was not uncommon to find parents who worked seven days a week tending to a family grocery store or a father bent over some cloak in a tailor shop for endless hours. And the parent today whose marginal income is increased by a second job—what about him?

The difference lies in the matter of commitment. If the commitment is truly toward a better way of life for the child, then the child senses it and derives gratification from the parent's efforts. But if the commitment only gains the father self-esteem, the child comes away with a feeling of playing only a minor role in his father's endeavors because the father's goals are selfish and have really little to do with the child's needs. What happens in a family when its father's needs go beyond the economic needs of the family? Although the case I have chosen may appear to be an extreme one, the lessons we can learn can well apply to a number of suburban families where the same basic difficulties jeopardize the child's emotional health.

No Time for Tests or Talk

I had occasion to see in consultation an industrialist who was asked by his family physician to see a psychiatrist because of a number of difficulties. Mr. E. K. was only thirty-nine, but on his way to an early grave. He had diabetes and paid scant attention to his dietary needs. So busy was he in pursuing his need to amass an industrial empire that he bluntly told his internist that he had no time to watch his diet and sometimes forgot to take his insulin. Test his urine with a tablet each day? Surely the doctor was mad for making such a request. Who had the time? See a psychiatrist? Who had the time? There was the new plant going up in Cleveland that required his attention.

Weeks later, when his wife brought to his attention the fact that their seven-year-old son was having difficulties in school, his answer could have been predicted. School was her area to take care of. His area was in gaining economic security for the family. Economic security? He already owned enough stocks and real estate to net him a handsome income without working.

And so it was left for Mrs. K. to take the initiative. A conference at school was arranged. The teacher informed Mrs. K. that Dennis was difficult to manage in class. He was bright but seldom completed his work. He always seemed to be trying to get teacher's attention in any way he could, even if it meant striking or pushing the boy or girl next to him. He didn't seem happy and the teacher commented on his appearing either depressed or angry. Mother was advised to seek help for him.

Mrs. K. reported this to her husband on his return from the midwest. He remained unimpressed. Only on her insistence that she would seek help herself did he agree to pursue the idea of consultation. At this time he made use of the referral made weeks ago by his doctor. He had his wife call and make an appointment. An arrangement to meet with the boy and his parents was met with resistance by Mr. K. He half-heartedly agreed to take his son, but arrived for the appointment with the excuse that Dennis had a bad cold.

When I first encountered Mr. and Mrs. K. in the waiting room, Mr. K. was shuffling through a sheaf of papers which he hurriedly threw into an attaché case as he and his wife came into my office.

Mr. K. took a seat farthest from my desk. A balding, short man, he looked older than his thirty-nine years. The seat he took, his businesslike manner, all indicated the approach he was to take about his and his son's problems. He was bright and articulate and I could have been drawn into a verbal sparring match. This is what happened when I first began my practice. I learned from experience that you can't help anyone unless they want to help themselves. It became apparent that Mr. K. had come with a closed mind and his trip to the office was to placate his wife. Mrs. K. sat close to the desk. She was a tall, strikingly attractive, well-groomed woman who spoke little. Her eyes seemed to do the talking in an almost pleading manner. She was asking for help and seemed so unable to cope with her husband, who obviously overwhelmed her with his verbal barrage filled with rationalizations. It is rather difficult to tell such a man, who seems to know so much, that in some areas he knows so little. Our session ended with the announcement that he was well aware of what was wrong with Dennis and that he felt the family could readily cope with the problem without any professional help. With that he arose, shook my hand and bade me goodbye. Mrs. K. was about to say something, but it ended with her following him out, her eyes still communicating her feelings of despair.

Hello ... Goodbye

The sometimes father like Mr. K. does not always merely say goodbye. Sometimes he will say, "Hello. Here is my child. Goodbye." He is the father who, like Mr. K., is very busy, but who admits that there are difficulties with his child. Reluctantly he offers the psychiatrist the child to treat, only he hasn't any time himself to participate actively in a treatment program. As far as he is concerned, there is nothing wrong with himself or his way of doing things. His business enterprises keep him in perpetual motion—by car, airplane, train, and boat. Sometimes a vehicle takes him in the direction of his home. When the pressures become very great he may even find the time to consult with his child's psychiatrist. He is happy to pay for his wife's psychiatric bills and all of his children's as well—only you must accept the fact that he is a hard man to see—or to reach.

Eventually the problems increase. The wife shows less patience in coping with the many problems of running a household. Often she finds herself short-tempered with the children. Then husband's argument is, "Here I am breaking my back to get you and the kids all the comforts of life and you have the nerve to complain. What ingratitude!"

All the luxuries of life, and somehow the children are starving. I have seen that it is difficult for such fathers to appreciate that their children want them as fathers—not as wealthy strangers who buy them off. It doesn't take long for the wife to tire of her jewels and furs and the children to look upon their expensive playthings as a poor substitute for the real thing—a real father—one who can play with his children with a ten-cent ball, not the one who has a bowling alley installed in the basement while he is off to Europe on another business trip.

Of Suburban Bondage

What of the wife of the sometimes father? Although married, she is almost a widow. The sometimes father is just as often a sometimes husband. Since all duties regarding caring for home and children are left entirely to her, she is often overwhelmed and her burdens are sometimes herculean. Living in the suburbs may have its virtues, but not when father is not there to actively participate with house and children. In the city, schools, libraries, friends, recreation, and churches are usually all within walking distance. In the suburbs it is usually the parents who must chauffeur children about, shopping is done by car, trips to the library or dentist are by car. Even to see a friendly face sometimes requires a car ride. Without a husband and father to talk to, to plan with, to share with, the routine duties of the suburban wife can become overwhelming and depressing. She pouts and complains and often the children become the recipients of her anger and frustration. That is when the child psychiatrist is often brought into the picture to try to explain to the sometimes father the concept of "buying time."

"Buying Time"

The businessman or professional who is so accustomed to dealing in concepts of selling for a profit or performing services for money can sometimes be approached with the concept of "buying time" for his family. It is essential for him to realize that his biggest investment is his family. You cannot have an emotionally healthy family if you don't invest your time in your wife and children.

I know from personal experience how easy it is to be lured into spending a few more hours at the office. Is it worth it? Absolutely not. An adult cannot recapture his childhood; a parent can never recapture the pleasurable hours he could have spent with his children. Sometimes, sibling rivalry being what it is, they can be agonizing hours. But often they are quite pleasurable and most essential for the child's mental health.

Only last week I had occasion to see a very disturbed boy. His father actually worked at his business from daybreak till late at night, seven days a week. It would not be correct to say that all of the boy's troubles could be traced to his father's business activities. But what his father, a wealthy man, said is worthwhile remembering—"I have so much and yet I have nothing."

The Edifice Complex

A phenomenon more readily seen in the suburbs than elsewhere is the edifice complex. This is when a house never becomes a home because mother or father or both insist that rooms be looked at or looked into, but never lived in. It is when gardens are made for show and not to be enjoyed by the children. Children in such homes walk about as though they are playing the game Simon says—"Hands in pockets place." Objects are not to be touched—they may be broken. Sofas are not to be sat on—they may be dirtied and worn. And grass is not to be played on—it may get trampled.

Little wonder such children suffer deprivation amid wealth. They rightfully feel that the parents show more concern for the possessions and furniture than they do for the children.

This is not to say that it is wise to have a toddler among expensive bric-a-brac. I am speaking of grown children who are not allowed to have guests over to their house for mother fears they will dirty the place. Or the father who breaks his back (or wallet) to build a fancy garden and insists the children play elsewhere. Can you picture several such families living near one another? Fortunately the condition is not too common. Having seen some children whose parents had the edifice complexes, I strongly urge any parent who places a possession first and his child's needs second to give some serious thought to the consequences.

The Absentee Mother

During the past generation we have seen a major revolution in the role of women in many countries of the world. In a matter of twenty years the number of married women who work has doubled. Not too many years ago a working married woman with children, whose husband worked, was looked upon as some sort of neurotic rebel who had no feeling for her family. In recent years, the upheaval in the role of women in our culture has been such that in some quarters it is the woman who has no job or interests outside her home who is looked upon as odd.

With more and more girls going off to college, many entering professions requiring years of study, there will be a rise in the number of mothers who find themselves occupied with some position outside the home. Does this mean an upheaval in the security of the intact family—an upheaval that will lead to instability for the children and consequent emotional illness? Not necessarily so.

We know that many a healthy child has grown up in a home where mother has worked. We also see those children who had suffered in homes where the mother worked. What makes for the difference? There are a number of factors to consider. What are these factors? What part do they play in how a child reacts to the absentee mother?

Needed: An Identity

A most important factor in the proper emotional development of children is their seeing, feeling, and accepting themselves as they truly are. This process is accompanied by their unconsciously copying themselves after their closest elders. We call this identifying. Ideally a boy should identify with his father, a girl with her mother. At a time when there is a cultural revolution in the role of women outside the home, we might expect some difficulty for children in properly identifying with their sex when they perceive the two roles as interchangeable. Yet this need not be so.

A mother happy in her role of wife who also takes on an added occupation or profession can well be seen and felt as the mother around the house. It is when the mother rejects herself as a woman and hence as a mother and therefore absents herself from the house—it is then that we can predict emotional difficulties for the children.

The Discontent

In every psychiatric office one can find an unhappy woman whose discontent stems from her difficulty in accepting herself as a woman. She feels incomplete. Marriage, motherhood, and even an occupation still leave her feeling discontent. She seeks and seeks and finds herself frustrated. In her home we do not find the harmony conducive to family well-being. The children feel the mother's unhappiness. Quite often there is open rivalry with the father. It seems as though the parents always seem to be singing the song Ethel Merman made famous in Irving Berlin's musical, *Annie Get Your Gun*. Some of the lyrics are: "I can do it better. . . . No, you can't. . . . Yes, I can . . . No, you can't. . . ."

Mother's unconscious need to be a man does not lead to fulfillment, no matter what she attempts. She still can't be a man. This is unlike the fulfillment attained by women who because of drive, training, and intellect desire to pursue a career outside as well as inside the home. She is happy—the husband doesn't feel rivalry for his male position, the children can still have a proper parental image to identify with.

Again, a Matter of Commitment

In discussing father's absence from the home, I spoke of a matter of commitment. What I said regarding the father and his commitment to his family or self is true for the mother as well. When a mother's commitment to outside work lets her family obligations become secondary, then this will be felt by the husband and children. Bitterness and bickering usually occur. Children readily feel the secondary role they are asked to play. They don't like it and begin to act up. A good example of this is seen in the chapter, "Kids Get Sick," where Elsa began getting "headaches" on school days as she felt her mother paid greater attention to her job as teacher for the "brain injured" than to Elsa.

A Matter of When and How

An important question for a mother thinking of working outside the home is "When is it least likely to have any harmful effects on the children?" The age of the children must be considered. At an early age a substitute mother must be sought and at some ages mother should be home if at all possible. What are these ages?

As I pointed out in an earlier chapter, it matters little to the infant during the first five months as to who is doing the holding, feeding, and diaper changing as long as the child feels secure. In the middle of the first year there is a radical change. The child becomes very much aware of the one person who is doing most of the caring. Of course, this is usually the mother. Often the child behaves as though hopelessly lost without her. A marked dependency has developed and is essential for proper mental growth. It is not wise and may be quite harmful for a mother to be absent for any length of time on a daily basis (or even on vacation, for example) until the child is capable of saying "Goodbye, mama" and not feeling overwhelmed by a sense of abandonment. This normally occurs at the age of about three when youngsters can begin to feel somewhat secure with their peers and mother-substitutes.

After the age of three it usually is much easier for a mother to leave the care of her child to a competent mother-substitute. Again, each child is unique and situations differ. Where monetary needs or a mother's sense of frustration with merely caring for the child and household chores become overwhelming, she might seriously consider getting out of the home to work, leaving the daily chores to some competent person, the mother doing a better job of mothering when she is at home.

Children in Parents' Clothing

Although the words "children in parents' clothing" may sound derisive, it is not so meant. Each and every one of us has our needs. Many are the needs we had as children. Unfortunately for some, circumstances make it such that needs that should have been abandoned with maturation still linger and interfere with the individual's role as parent. It does not mean that the parents are "bad" or "irresponsible" or "lazy." These are lay terms and do not help us to understand the basic factors that make the parents behave as they do. How do some parents act out the continued conflicts of childhood that have not been resolved? What makes for an adult? Who are these parents that live in an adult world but nevertheless show some childish behavior? What do I mean by children in parents' clothing?

True parenthood is not a passive phenomenon. It is a living, active, and dynamic process. Young children are too weak to take. Parents must therefore give if the child is to survive. The newborn would perish if he were not actively fed by an adult. This is not true of many lower forms of animals, who manage to survive without an active role by a parent. But not so in the human. Just as we must nourish physically, so a child must be nourished emotionally. Being a parent requires giving of oneself—to one's marriage partner and to one's children. This giving of oneself is not easily done unless one is truly an adult. Age here does not matter. A teen-age mother can be more of an adult with her children than a forty-year-old housewife.

What are the factors that have potentially good parents hold on to some need that has them behave like children? In my introduction I spoke of how some unconscious needs of ours come into conflict with the needs of our children. It is then that we find the children in greater difficulty. Since the parents' troubles are based on unconscious conflicts—by definition they are not seen or understood—the problems remain unresolved. Perhaps we can learn something by discussing some examples of such conflicts.

Mama Doll

Years ago, while in training, I had occasion to see a boy, Jacob, eight years old, brought to the clinic because of underachievement and aggressive behavior at school. I shall never forget the impression Jacob's mother made upon me. It was ten o'clock in the morning. There was Mrs. E., in a shimmering sequin dress, rhinestone earrings almost reaching to her shoulders, makeup applied with great care. Her attractiveness seemed rather overshadowed than enhanced by her costume. She had obviously come to impress us.

Jacob was the older of two children. His sister, Janice, was five. Jacob's teacher had insisted that he see a psychiatrist because of his continued harassment of the other children. The teacher at times kept him after class and when the two were alone he was an angel. But put him in with his peers and—wham! He would be jostling and pulling, punching and pinching, kicking and bickering. He was always in the midst of difficulties and had an excuse for anything that happened. It was always the next guy who started it. Academically, teacher felt he could perform much better. At home Jacob showed his dislike for Janice, and mother attributed any difficulties to normal sibling rivalry.

After several interviews it was decided that both child and mother be seen individually in treatment. Jacob was to be treated by another doctor and his mother was to be seen by me.

Mrs. E. was a warm, friendly person who was an only child. At the age of eleven her father, a violinist, suddenly died of a heart attack. Mrs. E. felt close to him and his loss was most traumatic for her. She continued her studies and mother and daughter continued living in the same house trying to overcome a loss both felt keenly. Mrs. E. remembered her father as "the most kindly . . . always bringing me presents . . . always complimenting me."

On graduation from high school Mrs. E. took a job as a secretary. Within a year she met and married Mr. E., a salesman for the firm. Mrs. E. had warm feelings for Mr. E. and particularly cherished his endearing name for her, "Doll." Within the year, Mrs. E. conceived but had a miscarriage. It seemed Mr. E. blamed himself for allowing her to work during her early months of pregnancy and insisted she stop working and remain at home. Although this caused a financial strain, Mrs. E. remained at home and soon conceived again. She described a most devoted husband "who waited hand and foot on me. I wasn't allowed to even wash a dish." Meals were often served to her in bed. And "Mama Doll" loved it. There wasn't anything within reason that Mr. E. would not do for her.

At Jacob's birth money was borrowed for a baby nurse so Mrs. E. could have her rest for at least a month. In the early months much of Jacob's care was left haphazardly to either some help or Mrs. E.'s mother, who usually worked as a saleslady. At times Mrs. E. wondered whether her husband sometimes felt little Jacob was too much of a burden for her. On learning of her second pregnancy, Mrs. E. again took to bed, again was waited upon, and Jacob's care was even more haphazard. Also, the father, faced with increasing financial burdens took on some extra work. Two new faces were introduced to Jacob when he was three, his sister and the new baby nurse. Mama was concerned with mama, papa with earning a living, and the nurse with little Janice. How did Jacob fit in? Not very comfortably.

In the ensuing years Jacob was pretty much on his own. With the growth of Janice, mother found herself feeling overwhelmed. By the time Jacob was six he was taking his own breakfast of cornflakes and milk and trudging to school, shoelaces untied, leaving his mother and sister sleeping soundly in the apartment.

As we worked together in treatment it developed that Mrs. E. found in her husband a lost father, and in a way, fortunately for her, he catered to her very much as her father had done years before. The difficulty was that in her continued need to take there was not enough of giving for the new children (i.e. Jacob and Janice) to feel their needs fulfilled.

With her own unconscious needs brought to the surface for her to see, Mrs. E. gradually found herself giving more to both Jacob and Janice.

In his own treatment, Jacob began to understand his anger towards Janice, his rival, and towards all who were rivals for either his mother or his teacher (i.e. substitute-mother). He was then better able to tolerate his impulses and reports from school showed good improvement in his relationship with his classmates.

The Professional Son-in-Law

In "Mama Doll" we have seen how the unresolved conflicts of a girl who lost her father prevented her from carrying on the normal demands of motherhood. In similar fashion this can occur in a man as well. Sometimes it ends with the young man becoming a professional son-in-law. What is a professional son-in-law? He is the man who is fortunate (or perhaps unfortunate) to have married a wealthy girl and has her "wear the pants." Not that marrying a wealthy girl has to be unfortunate. But there are times when poverty or deprivation, such as the loss of a parent in childhood, can be powerful forces which can make a man carry into his adult life the unconscious need to be cared for. Such a man, when he marries the wealthy girl, fathers the children but leaves most power and decisions to the wife or father-in-law. In essence, he remains the little boy who has a mother and father who care for him.

As stated earlier, a most important developmental process in a child's life is the process by which a child identifies with someone close to him. This process is never really thought about—it is unconscious. To be happy and emotionally stable a boy must identify with a male figure, hopefully his father, and a girl must identify with a female, hopefully her mother.

Where the mother is the powerful figure in the houshold, boys are faced with an enormous problem. On the one hand their minds seek to identify with their father, but they would also like to identify with a source of strength (i.e. the powerful parent), in this case the mother. What to do? Be a man or woman? Quite a dilemma!

Who Am I? What Am I?

Not infrequently, such a child, during adolescence, when it is normal for great emotional rumbling to occur, has greater difficulty in adjusting. "Who am I? What am I?" are questions more difficult for him to resolve satisfactorily. In seeking answers to questions he can only feel and not fully comprehend, he often turns to alcohol and drugs.

In situations where these problems exist it becomes necessary to help the entire family. It is important for the mother to understand her own role and her unconscious need to be the dominant partner, for the father to understand his past which has him be passive in his relationships to his wife and children, and for the child to be able to establish a proper identity and image of himself.

Success in the Slums

In a world filled with wars, bigotry, and hate, there are many children and their parents who lead a more difficult life because they are often a minority living in crowded, poverty-stricken neighborhoods—slums.

For more than a decade I have been directly involved in the treatment of emotional problems of children and adults living in the slums of Brooklyn, New York. I believe I have learned something from my work and I should like to share some of these observations and offer some counseling to the much-harried parents of such children.

It would be foolish of me to think that I could in a few words (or even volumes) present the multitude of problems and solutions for those living in slums. But we can take a look at some of the more pressing difficulties as they involve the child.

The Unit of Power

Much has been written and said recently regarding power. Such terms as black power, white power, and economic power have been bandied about. These are the words of the adult. To the child—any child—the unit of power—that power of how we feel about ourselves, the power of emotional stability, has never been measured in terms of color, be it black, white, or gold. If we were to look for the one important criterion of how much power is amassed by the child, then we would have to look at the power of a family. It is the intact family that is the unit of power to the child. It does not matter what color he is nor where he lives. There never has been, nor will there ever be, a substitute for the power in a child's emotional development that is derived from his being a part of an intact family. Give him the warmth and security of a loving mother and father, and all hell can break loose around him. He will remain secure. Take away one of his parents and don't give him a substitute and you destroy whatever security the child has. He is then naked to the world, in a position to be ravaged by what the child, any child, of any background, feels is a hostile world.

My former high school teacher, Sam Levenson, states it quite well in his autobiography, *Everything But Money*. The *everything* he refers to is a family. Only a family can plan, can have hope, can have goals. I am not blind to the struggles of our Negroes where hope is quashed each time they try to break some segregated stronghold. But if these segregated strongholds are to be broken, if the children are ever to break out of the slums, it can only be done by the power of a family—never singly, never alone, rarely with only a fragment of a family.

Some who read the above will say, "What do you really know about living in a slum?" My answer is simple—I think I know children, whether they live in a slum or in the lap of luxury. The factors which lead to delinquency, crime, and addiction among our older children are the very same factors among the wealthy who have never seen a slum. Why are some wealthy children found to be thieves or addicts or school dropouts? For the same reasons some children of the slums have these difficulties—primarily the lack of a healthy intact family. Show me a healthy intact family and I'll show you power. Show me an emotionally healthy child who has the power to break out of a slum, and I'll show you an intact family. Show me a broken home with no parent-substitute, and I'll show you fear and weakness that is covered with anger and hatred.

"The Man"

The anger and hatred that spills over into the streets by gangs of adolescents is often the outcry of the grown child who has been neglected in the past. It is little wonder that this anger and hatred becomes focused on authority figures such as the police officer ("The Man"). It is my feeling, based upon my experience with these adolescents, that often it is the real father against whom this hatred is really felt. The father, who abandoned the now-troubled child or treated the child harshly, is both loved and hated, wanted and rejected.

A Need to Belong

Each and every child has a need to belong. That need is satisfied by first belonging to a set of parents or substitute parents. It is only after that very basic need is satisfied that a child can feel he belongs to a group—be it a classroom, a community or a nation. If the need is not satisfied, the child will be certain to manifest emotional difficulties. It can be a feeling of worthlessness associated with depression, it can be anger that has him strike at all the people about him. It can certainly lead to his doing poorly in school. In the older child it will show itself in the child's anger at authority and society. Riots and bloodshed are the raw results.

Fairly typical of these children is a boy we shall call James. He was eight years old when he was referred to our clinic. Looking at his clinic chart we read the following: ". . . referred by the school guidance counselor because he sits quietly but not attentively in his class, and seems to be withdrawn into a world of his own. At other times he loses his temper and fights furiously with his classmates. At other times he . . . will laugh uncontrollably or call out words such as 'tuna-fish' or 'potatoes' . . . that have no connection with the lesson at hand, and he laughs at himself. His achievement at school is unsatisfactory. Patient's mother states that if he feels he has been slighted he must get revenge or he goes to pieces, cries, and has temper tantrums. Patient's mother is unmarried and has four children all by different fathers. . . . The mother left the patient when he was eight months old and came to New York. Three months later she returned . . . he had lost weight and seemed to have some stomach trouble. Patient has had eneuresis since childhood. He has always bitten his nails and grinds his teeth at night. He was never a warm or affectionate child, and never smiles. There have always been difficulties in school since the first grade. He will not let anyone touch him. He does not get along well with other children in the neighborhood and is friendly with one child. He speaks very seldom to his mother. He sleeps and eats well but does not cooperate with the mother."

On the mental examination the doctor wrote, "This is a well-developed eight-year-old boy who comes hesitantly to the interview. He refuses to sit in the chair or take off his coat. Frequently his body becomes rigid. He is negativistic, although it is possible to establish contact with him with great difficulty. Speech is sparse. Frequently he is mute. He has to be drawn out by giving him affection and kindness. The effect is blunt and inappropriate . . . after a great amount of attention was spent on him he began to play ball with the examiner and refused to leave and go back to his mother."

A Glimmer of Hope

James was accepted for treatment and was seen once a week for forty-five minutes by a resident psychiatrist. We begin to see the glimmer of hope, as a healthy relationship, the first for James, is established with his doctor. Complete progress notes were kept and the following are the doctor's notes in their entirety for the sixth, seventh, and eighth visits with James. It shows us how a psychiatrist can assist a child to develop a healthy and trusting relationship essential for his emotional development.

SESSION VI

Patient arrived early and while waiting for me he asked the clerk at the desk if he could go into the toy room and by the time I came he had a truck with which he was playing. (This was the first time that he ever spoke to the hospital personnel.)

I remarked to James about the truck and he pointed to the toy room. He seemed quite happy rolling the truck to and fro. He stopped, looked up at me and held up two fingers. I said this is the second week and it is time for an ice cream. He shook his head. I asked him about school, he said he missed one day and doesn't deserve ice cream. I asked him to tell me about it. He said he forgot. I said he must remember something about it. He said that one of the boys started to fight with him and he kicked him back but that he had been trying not to have fights or be in trouble all week. I said it was excellent that he had tried so hard and that sometimes it takes a while before he could control himself and that he should have an ice cream anyway for having tried. He said, "But if I go for an ice cream I can't play here." That's true, which do you want? "I want both." You can have both but only one at a time. "O.K., ice cream today and play next week." We got dressed and we left to buy ice cream. On the way over he said that I should order it. However, at the last moment at the counter of the store he ordered the ice cream himself, with a paper on top. I asked about the paper and he said he wanted to eat it only while walking with me in the hospital grounds. While walking in he asked why did I not buy an ice cream for myself. I said that I am smoking my pipe and I enjoyed that. While he was eating his ice cream tears ran down his cheeks and he started to walk away from me on the grass. I followed him and pointed out that he was crying. He said, "It's nothing, it's only tears." He added, "It's because it is so cold." I pointed out that it really was not so cold that day and maybe it was because of how he felt. He said nothing and I said maybe you are sad. He shook his head, no. Maybe it is because you're happy. He shook his head, yes. When we returned to the clinic he opened the elevator door and operated the elevator in the building. He offered me a lick of his ice cream. I thanked him but did not take it. He asked if there was still time to play. I pointed out that there was very little time left but that we would be able to play next week. While finishing his ice cream he said, "In three more weeks if I go to school I will get another ice cream?" I said yes.

SESSION VII

Patient missed the week before. His mother phoned in saying he was sick. James ran to meet me as I got off the elevator and said, "I couldn't come last week, I was sick, I had trouble with my ear." I said I was sorry to hear that and how does he feel now. He said O.K. and said he wants to play with a painting set. He began painting animal pictures. He seemed relaxed and spoke spontaneously in full sentences pointing only rarely when he wanted something. He drew various animals and named them. He turned to me and said, "You draw some too." I took up a brush and both of us began painting. I began printing the name *James* on one of the sheets of paper. He picked up the paper, held it, and asked if he could write his second name. He printed it with my help and seemed quite pleased. After that he began drawing more animals and seemed quite satisfied after having completed each one. He soon got tried of this and I asked him how he felt about missing last week's session. He said he was sad about it but he was happy today. He said that school was good last week and that he gets an ice cream next week if everything is good. At the end of the session he asked if I wanted one of his pictures. I took one and thanked him. While leaving he pointed to his shoes and said, "Look at my nice new shoes." I agreed that they were nice.

(Mother states that patient has been getting along much better with his siblings and his schoolmates as well. On the one morning that he was sent home he begged his mother to be permitted to return to the afternoon session. She finally allowed him to go and patient was able to remain at school without any trouble.)

SESSION VIII

When I went into the room the patient was looking out the window with a pair of binoculars. I asked him what he was looking for. He said, "Nothing." (His mother told me later that he was looking through the binoculars out the window to watch me come up the walk.) He said, "Today I get my ice cream. I wasn't sent home all week and my teachers were good to me." I said that this was very good and I was glad to hear that. While we were dressing to go out he said he wanted something else instead. "An ice cream with strawberries on top of it." A sundae? "Yes." I'd like to buy you that, James, but I can only buy you something that costs the same amount as an ice cream. "O.K. I want an ice cream." While we were walking to the store I put my arm around him and he moved close. He asked about a new building that was going up and wanted to know if it was going to be the same as this one. I asked him why and he did not answer. In the store he ordered a vanilla ice cream and this time he began licking it on the street. He did not talk, but then said, "Would you like to look through my binoculars?" I thanked him and made some comment about some things I saw through them. He was quiet for a long time while eating and I asked him what he was thinking about. "About not being absent from school and listening to my teacher. I want to learn to read." I said that by going to school regularly and working with his teachers this can be done. He then said, "I have fights with my sister." I asked him what happens. He said that his sister bothers him when he wants to watch T.V., so "I kick her." I said I could understand him getting angry with her when she does that and I wondered whether there was something else he could do to stop her. He said, "Nothing." I asked if he was sure and he said, "Tell her to stop bothering me." I said, "Yes, it is so good for you to be able to say this." He said, "Next time she bothers me I'll kick her, I mean I'll tell her to stop." He then went on to say that Mommy sometimes makes him do things he doesn't like, like sweeping the floor. I asked him what he does. He said, "I don't do it or I fight because I don't like it." I asked him, "Do you ever tell her?" He said, "Sometimes." What happens? "Sometimes she says O.K., go play, and sometimes she says you have to do it anyway." I said that he can see that by talking to her sometimes he can do what he wanted to and sometimes he has to do what he is told. When he got upstairs he asked, "When do I get my next ice cream?" I said, "In four weeks." He said, "Four weeks is too long, I can't wait." I said, "Four weeks is only one week more than you have waited already. Do you think you can wait just one week longer?" He said, "You might not be here." Why? "It is so very long from now." I reassured him that I would be here. He said, "I'm afraid you will leave me." I told him that I liked him and that I would not leave him. I also pointed out that I have a holiday for three weeks in August, that I would tell him long in advance and that I would be back after that as well.

It was time to end the session and he said, "Do I have to leave now? I want to stay here." I pointed out that he would have to leave but that I would be back. He said, "Can I take a toy home and bring it back next week?" I said I didn't know, I would have to ask the chief of the hospital and tell him next week. He said, "I want it now." I said I couldn't give it to him on my own, that the chief is not here now, but that I would definitely let him know next week. He left rather discontented.

Forty-Five Minutes for a Life

Just forty-five minutes a week made an enormous difference for James. His life began to change. Reports from school indicated a marked change in his behavior. He was no longer aggressive because he was no longer as angry. Those forty-five minutes a week gave him what he most needed—self-respect, hope, a chance to identify with a father figure, a chance to understand his fears and hopes. We can appreciate his need to belong when he expresses his fear of the doctor leaving him.

At the end of the year the doctor had finished his training in child psychiatry, and treatment of James was ended. Although James had done extremely well and was placed in a class for brighter students, the chronic upheaval at home was again to take its toll.

A year later a social worker noted:

"For the past two or three months James has been restless in school . . . [his mother] feels her sister's presence in the household has aggravated James. This sister came from the south with her one child and joined the household. James complains that his aunt favors her own child and is not fair to the others. Also, James has voiced his dislike of different men coming to see his aunt."

The Return of Silent Anger

The problem of further treatment for James became my problem, as I had become the director of the children's clinic. The needs of the vast number of children like James could not be met by the limited staff we had. I saw James and it was readily apparent that his depressed sullenness covered a boiling cauldron of silent anger. He felt lost, and anyone sitting with him could feel his anguish. A request to the

Department of Welfare that they make some provision to assist James in continuing treatment with his former doctor at a very low fee was met with a "No." Although my job was essentially administrative, I decided to include James in a group of children I was treating with medication. Most of them had brain damage or were psychotic. I saw him for brief periods when it became apparent that no other therapist was available.

James kept his appointments, always coming alone. Because of his restlessness in class, a mild tranquilizer was prescribed. He didn't take the medication. In his silent way he was telling me that a pill was a poor substitute for a parent. Months later I felt gratified to receive the following letter from his teacher:

DEAR DR. FASS:

James has shown some improvement since you have been treating him. He appears to be much calmer and does not become angry or excited when the class is engaged in work he cannot do or does not like. He asks for assistance when he is doing his assignments. On occasion, he will raise his hand to volunteer an answer. He does not call out or disturb the class the way he formerly did.

He gets along better with the other children during class games. He is an excellent ball player. He is willing to obey the decisions of the umpire. He often smiles and tells a joke.

There are times when he pushes or strikes other children. He often has trouble coming up from the school yard. The boys complain that he hits them. James always says that he is only playing with them.

His homework has improved. His assignments are completed and he is anxious for me to see his work. His handwriting has improved a great deal.

James went to the World's Fair with the class. His conduct was satisfactory. He was interested in the exhibits and he has drawn many pictures of what he saw.

I hope this information will be of some assistance to you. If I can be of any help in the future, please let me know.

Very truly yours. . . .

James was eight years old when he first came to our clinic. Today he is going on sixteen and still comes to talk with me. It's been a long haul for him. He will tell me how he'd like an expensive pair of shoes his mother feels she can't afford. But this is a quite small deprivation when we compare it to being deprived of a father, a man he can communicate with, look up to, and hope to emulate.

Preventing Perpetuation

James and the thousands of boys like him grow up. They become men physically. But the emotional damage they suffered leaves them in a poor position to enter into a healthy emotional relationship with a woman. They become fathers, but often their self-image is so weak that should they marry they often find it so difficult to relate to the world about them that they, too, go off and do what was done unto them—they abandon their children.

If children like James and James's children are to survive in a healthy manner a great deal must be done and done immediately. It is essential that we recognize the problem that exists and attack it on all fronts—educationally, economically, socially, and medically.

EDUCATIONALLY

It is not only important that James's mother learn the necessity of a father for James. It is vitally important that all elements of society recognize this need and work together towards attaining such a goal. For example, there are homes that I know of where fathers are seldom seen, because the mother is on welfare and there is the fear that the payments would be stopped or reduced if a man were found on the premises. It is utterly preposterous to subsidize a fatherless home and penalize a home with a father. It would be far better for welfare departments to gear their efforts toward attaining an intact family. If people are on welfare we should make it materially advantageous that there be intact families. This would pay off handsomely in mentally healtheir children. Even the taxpayer would have to agree when a generation later the welfare rolls diminish rather than increase as they have been doing year after year.

ECONOMICALLY

It is essential that a father have a decent job where he can earn enough to enable him to hold his head erect and feel that he can support his children.

SOCIALLY

A family must have a decent place to live in. A nation such as ours that can give billions to any country that smells a Communist in its midst ought to be able to finance the building of houses so a family can live together decently.

MEDICALLY

The forty-five minutes a week that meant so much for James should be extended to the great number of other children who so desperately seek help. That will take time and money. But it will be well worth our effort to increase by many-fold the psychiatric facilities we now have so as to be able to reach the thousands like James who receive no help at all.

A new approach in community mental health is also necessary. We cannot possibly immediately amass the army of trained personnel that is so urgently required. What can be done on a large, organized scale is being done in an unorganized and small way. I am referring to the use of young college people and elderly people who desire to help with deprived children.

A large number of children should be reached on a one-to-one basis. A young man of twenty could do wonders spending several hours a week with a boy, building a model airplane, or going bowling or to the zoo, or just talking over an ice cream cone. It will give each a stake in the other's life and the communication can have lasting beneficial results for both.

A young college girl or a woman at any age could well assist in giving some love and attention to the daughter of a harried mother living in the slums.

In an organized manner, through the facilities of a community mental health program, in conjunction with an antipoverty program and with the cooperation of our urban universities and colleges, a pyramid system can be used to help the deprived child of the slums. Utilizing a team of psychiatrists, psychologists, social workers, and teachers, college students can learn about child development and thus be in a position to better contribute to the emotional welfare of their own future children and to the emotional nourishment of today's deprived children. Such courses and field work participation could become a part of most students' curriculum. The older, more affluent, and hopefully more sophisticated college youth can then develop a sense of participation in the welfare of those who are less fortunate. In later years, sitting in a position of power in law, medicine, politics, education, and industry, many will feel the need to continue to participate in the growth of these deprived children. The children of the slums will have the opportunity to communicate in a healthy manner with those who have a goal, a sense of purpose, and a future.

The wealth of any nation rests with its people. We usually think of people as adults. But it is the child who becomes the adult and what he becomes will depend on what adults do to him and for him. Abandon him and he will feel like nothing and contribute nothing. Nourish him and he will feel like something and contribute something.

Forty-five minutes a week can save a life. We have the funds; we have the people; and there are the children so urgently waiting. What are we waiting for?

Scream Along with Me

How can children in the slums be shielded from the frustration, bitterness, and despair that is the lot of their parents? A most difficult task, but not an impossible one.

Bitterness and despair often lead to frustration and anger. Years of deprivation have left some adults without hope, without a goal, and with only a legacy of hate. Their very existence seems to feed on this hatred for society. No one and nothing is good any more. They preach hatred and violence and cry out for others to join them in purposeless anger. Their cries are screams of anguish and hate, not of hope or of plans.

Children exposed to such preachings of hopelessness and hate will become anxious, because children fear the consequences of hate.

However bleak the surroundings, children must be fed with love and hope. When there are parents, love and hope can exist despite the cries of hate and despair. Parents who join in screaming along and spouting hate do their children a grave injustice. A child who is taught to hate will experience fear and anxiety.

Instant Einstein

Instant coffee, instant tea, and now instant Einstein. There are many books, kits, and manuals on the market today that are supposed to help each parent make his child into an instant Einstein. What they really can do is:

1—Make their inventors rich.

2—Make you poorer.

3—Make you a boastful bore at a social gathering.

4—Give your child something to forget.

5—Give your child the beginning of an emotional block toward learning.

Recently I was at a gathering where a mother brought along her two-year-old son. Proudly she removed a set of index cards from her purse and proceeded to have her child read such words as STOP, GO, TURN. Instead of sharing in this mother's bliss, I felt pity for the child, who had a fifteen-year wait for his driver's license test so he could make use of the words he had learned. More than that, I pity the parents who have such an overriding need to push the child into performing years before he is ready. Before he is presented with the task of reading, a child should first master the first and most important means of communication—speech.

Some years ago many parents felt obligated to start their young on some musical instrument. How proud many of them were when their six- and seven-year-olds tinkled at the piano keys and scratched at their violins. But how many of these children enjoyed what they were learning and carried it through into later years? Very few. Today we often hear a mother's complaint about how much money was spent on her child's musical lessons and how wasteful it had been. Or I see a young adult who describes the agony of being pushed into a learning process he had no interest in. Hopefully we do not do the same with reading.

Learning can and should be an enjoyable experience for children. Anyone who spends but a few minutes with a youngster finds himself bombarded with questions and realizes how a child's quest for answers is ceaseless. They hunger for knowledge. They want to know. We can, as parents, help them learn. What do we do and what don't we do? Let's begin with looking at our own needs regarding our children's intellectual abilities.

Genius Is Not Happiness

So many parents want their child to be a genius. Why? Do they equate genius with happiness or success? If so, they are mistaken. Too many geniuses are not happy people. I am not saying that a genius can't be happy. I do know that the feeling of happiness is found at all levels of intellectual functioning. If our goal as a parent is to set out to have a superior child, then the result will probably be a child who is superior—superior in the number of neurotic conflicts. If our goal is to make sure that he develops a superior mind so that he gets a superior education so that he will then earn lots of money, we are again on the wrong path. Too many millionaires have committed suicide—also too many college kids who have been pushed beyond their endurance. Our goal should always be one of having happy children—happy in what he is doing, happy in what he is learning. Some educators and parents may take issue with this and point out that some things must be learned though they may not make the child happy. What things? Like algebra to a bright, artistically inclined fourteen-year-old girl who hates it, never really needs it for the future, but only needs it to qualify for a diploma? Criteria for graduation and diplomas were established in the distant past and no one seems to dare ask why. When will we all—parents and educators—wake up to the fact that each child is different and happiness can never be measured by how much unnecessary information is stored by the hypothalamus of the brain?

If the child hungers for knowledge, then why do we find

some children not learning? Why the underachievers? There is no answer that will hold true for all children with learning difficulties. Some children may have perceptual difficulties; that is, the brain and sensory organs, such as the eyes, are not working in proper harmony. One such condition is known as dyslexia. The child cannot read properly because the image of the printed word is not recorded properly in his brain. Conditions where there are such perceptual difficulties can often be remedied with professional help.

A greater percentage of children, however, have learning difficulties based on emotional difficulties. It may be a child who experiences deprivation at home. A sick parent, parents quarreling or divorced, financial distress, are but a few of the situations that can occur to have the child experience learning difficulties. The child's mind may be too overwhelmed with the crisis at hand, or be filled with fantasies in an effort to escape the crisis.

Some of the difficulties are unavoidable. Others, such as when a child meets with the sheer inability to handle a particular subject or where there has been too much destructive criticism, are situations which parents can avoid or take a hand in remedying.

Creating the Proper Environment

To learn is to grow. If we look at a growing plant a most complex phenomena, photosynthesis, takes place using the simple elements of water, oxygen and sunlight. In similar fashion, what simple elements are necessary for the complicated process of learning?

1—Relatively happy parents who like to learn. Children are the world's greatest mimics. They imitate their parents in countless ways. Parents who like to learn will have newspapers, books, and magazines which they will be reading. Even our eighteen-month-old Amy will take a magazine, look into it (though upside down) and smile at me as she shows me that she is doing what I am doing.

2—Parents who will take the time out of their busy schedules to answer questions and do the things that their child wants to do—even though it was answered or done before with an older child. Children will love museums—if the museum has the things they are interested in seeing. Never try dragging a child to some exhibit or museum because you think he should want to see it.

Here again our best efforts may not have the desired results. I thought that surely my sons, then aged five and seven, would enjoy seeing a large boat show. But they quickly tired, were bored and asked to return home. My mistake was in taking them at too early an age to a show I was primarily interested in. The following year when they asked to go along to a medical convention I had my doubts as to the outcome. But thanks to the drug company which gave out a small doctor's bag and the hundreds of drug companies which handed out free samples, they exclaimed, "Gee, Dad, we had the best time of our lives."

—If they're interested in reptiles or guns, then take them where they may see such things or where some written material is available. If they can't read yet, then do take the time out to read about their interests to them. This is a most important motivating factor in their desire to learn to read.

4—Do allow them to follow through (within reason) on their curiosity that so often ends up in a mess that requires some cleaning—little girls in the kitchen, boys with their homemade chemistry sets of rubbing alcohol, bicarbonate of soda, talcum powder, etc.

5—Do show enthusiasm and approval of their simplest efforts. They want so much to please us. I remember my oldest daughter beaming with delight as my wife removed a work of art from an easel in our living room and replaced it with Sharon's painting of a winter scene done at nursery school. Her painting stayed on the easel for months, in a place of honor for us all to enjoy—particularly Sharon.

If criticism of a child's learning or school work is necessary, do make it constructive criticism that will motivate, not hinder, the very process you are trying to further. Don't compare a child's abilities, efforts, or work to yours or his sibling's or classmates'. Criticism should always be interwoven with acceptance. Not an easy task, but one that is possible and essential for parents and teachers. You can gain the child's cooperation if acceptance is there and added to it are suggestions for doing better. But simply criticizing is equal to rejection, and the child then has to build defenses against this hurt feeling. One common defense is not trying to do the work lest the result again end in criticism (rejection). Somehow, it is easier for the child to accept the rejection due to not trying than the rejection of an attempt. Another factor is the child's responding in kind. Rejected for what he has done, he will reject the rejector and all that is associated with him.

The Rituals and Trappings
of Civilization

The infant, the little animal, is accepted in the nude, full of feces and fury. A civilized citizen is expected to know which fork he must use for pickled herring, how a table is set, on which side of the street he walks while escorting a lady so that mud is not splattered upon her, and whether a button-down shirt is appropriate for a formal affair. How do we get the little animal to be a civilized citizen in a manner compatible with healthy upbringing and not go gray or bald in the process?

Relax!

As with the case of threatening habits, it is important that parents be objective in their attempts to produce a civilized citizen. Too often I have seen a parent more concerned about what will be thought of him, not only of his child, because of how he grows his hair or wears his clothes. The word here too is: Parents, relax! We can all smile together at a comment laughingly made by one mother: "Last year I couldn't get him to comb his hair. This year I can't get him away from the mirror." In other words, in most instances it is a matter of time. Time to learn, time to adjust to the many demands of living in a civilized society.

Wash and Weary

As a father, I too would like to have my children looking fairly clean and neat. Frankly, I wouldn't like them to look dirty and disheveled and have their teachers exclaim, "What can you expect? Their father is a psychiatrist." So I admit we've had our fair share of fussing over washing and brushing teeth.

Some children take readily to bathing and some see it as an unnecessary evil to be shunned. Perhaps some of the latter have hides that are literally more sensitive to temperature changes. We don't know what makes one child seek a bath and another cry out as though it were a torture rack. Where it is likened to medieval torture, my feelings are to forget the ritual of the daily bath and try again. It isn't wise to make the situation into a power struggle. Of course, the parent can always win, but is it worth it? I think not. Truthfully, a little dirt behind one's ears has never caused an illness. Some people have lived healthy, happy lives thinking of water as a necessity for growing good grapes and nothing more.

Ties and Ties

Some schools demand that all their boys from tots to teens wear ties and other "appropriate attire"—usually a sports coat. Girls, too, in many schools must often appear in "appropriate attire"—school uniforms. Perhaps this uniformity of uniforms helps the compulsive administrator feel things are under control. It doesn't matter to the child if he wears a piece of silk around his neck. What does matter very much are the ties he feels with his family and those around him. It hurts to see some of the children in private boarding schools where uniformity is a way of life. They wear their coats and ties with such perfect correctness. Their manners are impeccable. But such emptiness inside! Not that private schools or wearing a tie and coat has anything to do with their feeling empty. But where the true ties of feeling are missing, then all the correct dress doesn't mean a damn. Some of these children who live at private schools feel quite correctly that they are there to be out of their parents' way. Under these circumstances the child will more readily fit into the pattern of life set forth by the school in his attempt to find acceptance. He wears his tie, but where is the tie he seeks?

Long Hair and Small Minds

A child's and adolescent's life is filled with shifting conformity and rebellion. When the child conforms, the adult feels secure. Let the child veer from the standards set up by adults and the adult is threatened by what seems to be rebellion. It's the old establishment being threatened by the new. Sometimes we become a little too threatened. Take the wearing of long hair, for example. From the way some school administrators have behaved, it would appear they felt threatened and anxious. Rather than try to understand a child's need for long hair, their reaction was one of sheer horror that ended in a number of student expulsions. Was it all necessary? Were the long-haired children disruptive to the teaching going on? Were they all beatnik rebels or C.I.A. agents trying to infiltrate the ranks of those who look like Bolshevik revolutionaries? Or are they, in fact, children trying to find themselves in a world of cockeyed standards? Or children who feel threatened if any part of their body is cut? Careful consideration will place the great majority of long-haired children in the latter categories. I wonder what some small-minded school principal would have said in the year 1868 had a boy appeared in class with a crew cut?

Shall We Dance?

I should like to say a few words about what I have observed regarding social dancing in children before adolescence. Girls normally mature faster than boys, physically and sexually. In a group of eleven-year-olds, the boys are usually shorter and some of the girls are beginning to show signs of sexual maturation. The boy often has to strain his neck to look at the girl, for should he stare blankly ahead he will be sure to embarrass the girl, whose budding breasts he faces. In children between the ages of five and ten, it is perfectly normal not to want to participate with the opposite sex in any endeavor.

So when it comes to dancing, many children are angry and

embarrassed. The teacher comes away thinking she has brought one of the social graces of civilization into the staid life of a child while on the road from little animal to civilized citizen. I think not. Better to leave the boys to their baseballs and marbles and the girls to their jump ropes. Let them get to the point of wanting to learn to dance—at their own pace—when it means something other than dancing to the tune of well-meaning but misguided parents and teachers.

"Thar He Blows!"

The child no sooner begins to enjoy the sounds and odors accompanying his expelling gas by either one of two orifices than he is quickly warned that such artistry is *verboten.* Granted that such behavior is best suited to the privacy of one's privy, what does one do when a child takes delight in a public display of his new-found accomplishment? Hit him? Send him from the table? Neither is necessary. What is desirable socially requires years of learning. Give your child a chance to learn. If adults around him have a certain set of standards, he will in due time emulate them. In all probability, without undue pressure, the parents' social standards at the dining table and elsewhere will become the child's standards.

The thought of writing on the subject of belching would have never occurred but for a boy I once saw. With tears he described his father's admonishment and his banishment from the dining table. "And it wasn't even loud," he tearfully concluded.

"Doesn't Everybody?"

A congressman is accused of using government money for his personal use. His defense? "Doesn't everybody?" A cadet at a military academy is caught cheating during an examination. His defense? "Doesn't everybody?" A man cheats on his income tax and/or wife. His defense? "Doesn't everybody?"

It amazes me to see the incredulous looks on parents' faces when they bring their children for consultation because of cheating and stealing. "How could this have happened to my child?" they ask. The answer is often not complex. How frequently has the parent played the game of "Doesn't everybody?"

Three weeks ago a boy of ten I was seeing for a brief therapy came in quite angry. "How come you don't want to help my parents? You're not good." Frankly, I was stunned until I was able to understand what he was referring to. The previous week his mother had requested that since they had major medical insurance that covered fifty per cent of treatment, I should merely write in twice the true number of visits so that they could then have full reimbursement. The boy's mother continued the argument, "But what do you have to lose? Everybody does it." After the mother's telephone request was met with a firm "No," my waiting room was empty at their next scheduled hour. A call to the home was met with the father's comment, "I don't like your attitude. We're not coming any more."

Several years ago I saw a young man expelled from school for embezzling school funds. One evening he walked into my office laughing. What was so funny? Several hours before his mother was teaching his younger brother how to drive. The boy hit an unoccupied parked vehicle. Mother's quick re-

135

sponse? "Fast, let's get out of here." This was quite humorous to a boy in treatment for his own past antisocial difficulties.

Developmental Honesty

An infant is neither born honest nor dishonest. I do not believe that any child might be "predisposed" to cheating, stealing, and delinquent behavior. Too much depends on what happens to him and around him.

It takes time for a child to develop a sense of honesty. In the early years, cheating and stealing are fairly normal. Some children below the age of about nine find it too intolerable to lose at any game. They will cheat or stop playing or change the rules in their favor. This behavior is seen so frequently one can consider it fairly normal. There is no reason to make any fuss or to admonish the child.

Stealing is also fairly common in many children below the age of ten, and more usually between five and eight. By ten it is fairly well established in a normal child's mind what is his and what is "theirs." He has also learned (hopefully) that it is quite improper to take what is not rightfully his. Where dishonesty and stealing occur in children beyond the age of ten, reasons can be found in the relationships and communication established between the child and those around him. There is absolutely no such thing as a "born thief," or "poor character" that is inherited. To repeat, no child has ever been born to cheat or steal. When the child beyond the age of ten performs some antisocial act, it then becomes essential that we and the child understand the meaning of this act.

Catch Me! Catch Me!

I should like to tell you a story about a fifteen-year-old boy that many of you will find difficult to believe. When I saw Eddie he was already on probation. He had been to court more times than some trial lawyers. His background and difficulties became fascinating to me. Eddie never saw his father. Shortly after he was conceived his father was sentenced to many years in prison. His mother grew to detest his father, and in the succeeding years she saw develop before her eyes "the image of his father." His mother found it difficult to face Eddie, so angry was she at the father.

As Eddie grew, his mother found herself wishing she had never conceived. More important, she believed that Eddie would be as like his father mentally as he was physically. So strong was this belief that mother often expressed it to her close relations. Somehow Eddie saw to it that his mother's predictions would come true. He only stole in front of policemen and store detectives!

Chores and Challenges

In some homes the question of a child's cooperation with household chores becomes an important issue in the relationship between the child and parents. If we were to look into a number of homes we would find marked differences existing regarding a child's duties. In some homes too much is demanded and the child meekly obeys or openly rebels. In other homes nothing is requested and the child seeks chores to do, or does nothing. Can any of this be understood? Yes, if we know all the facts in the particular home. It might help us to understand the problem if we discuss some of the factors.

Contentment and Cooperation

I have attempted to show how each child is unique and how in the life of each child there are periods of stability and periods of stress. We can therefore readily understand that a request to do some household chore could be met with active cooperation during a period of quiescent contentment or with a rebellious "No" during periods of stress. Let us again realize that for some children it seems that life is almost always one of stress and all one hears are rebellious "No's." Does it necessarily mean that the cooperative child is mentally healthier and will be a more responsible adult? And that the rebellious child is sick and will never be a responsible adult? Absolutely not.

Many a girl has grown up with her mother standing by and wringing her hands in despair as she tries to teach her daughter the basic necessities of household work. Somehow she does find a husband, raises a flock of healthy children, runs a nice home, and mama goes away wondering how such an uncooperative, rebellious girl developed into a capable mother and wife.

A Child's Needs

Children are so wrapped up in their own needs that the needs of the parents become quite unimportant to them. Asked to go to the store on an errand, the child might wonder why he had to be the one to be chosen. Why not his brother? Or father? Or mother? Why me? Here again it is best for all if we can hold back any explosive feelings and question why the child feels the way he does. There is no such thing as a lazy child. Temporarily troubled? Probably. But never lazy. Rebellious? Could be. Again, why? Often we can't get to the cause and we feel quite frustrated. It is then best to accept the fact that children, more than adults, have their ups and downs, periods of cooperation and periods of negativism. And all the hollering in the world will not really alter the situation. It usually makes it worse.

Any Help Wanted

Before we put up a "Help Wanted" sign for our children, we have to have an "Any Help Wanted" sign. Any help means just that. It means that we allow our eager four-year-olds to help us wash our car, although anyone who has done so knows the mess that will develop. It means that we don't criticize the mess our three-year-old daughter makes when she heleps her mother bake a cake. It means that we unflinchingly accept the help our young children so often eagerly give. Children love to do what we are doing. Begin criticizing how poorly they do it and you are certain to have an older child (now better coordinated and more capable) say no to your request in later years. Somewhere in his mind is stored the memory of rejection and pain when he did try to help.

How Much?

Some parents feel they do so much for their children that they are shocked to have their child ask, "How much do I get for doing it?" "Why, the ingrate!" they may exclaim.

I see nothing wrong with using small amounts of money as an incentive if that is what the child requests, particularly if they are chores that are normally paid for.

Last summer I was ready to change my mind about this. I was clearing a wooded area so that my children and their friends could have more room to romp around. There were quite a few weeds and stooping down was tiring for me. I asked my sons to help unearth them. "How much?" Some parents might feel that since the project was for their benefit they should have done it without the "How much?" But in the past they were paid for helping to clear leaves and weeds and I saw nothing wrong with compensating them for the task. We agreed on one cent a weed—stem and roots. Two hours later I held my head as they brought over a bushel-basket full and counted, one, two, three—all the way to eleven hundred and fifty-three. Eleven dollars and fifty-three cents! Child labor? They seemed more like labor barons. They looked at me, and, sensing what I was thinking, Barry exclaimed, "You promised!" I had, and I had to pay.

How Come?

How come when he's away he even scrubs the toilet? "How come?" A question many parents ask, particularly of children who have been to camp or lived away from home at some time. Why does the child seem more cooperative away from home? The answer lies in the different relationships that exist outside the home. There is usually less anger and fewer feelings of rivalry outside the home. The child seeks acceptance in his new environment and will more readily follow the rules and regulations.

Friends and Enemies

As the child matures he gropes about him, encountering young people like himself. His feelings toward his peers are like a shifting kaleidoscope. A friend of one day may be someone to be shunned the next day. Bosom buddies are no longer even buddies. Or one day he walks hand in hand with someone he swore only yesterday was the "worstest person in the whole world."

An adult would be considered fickle by such behavior. In a child's life it is quite normal. It is therefore wisest to stand back and permit such goings-on. Pressuring a child to befriend someone because you happen to be good friends with the child's parents is not wise. Or making enemies with the parents of your child's "enemy of the day" is wrong. The next day you might be shocked to see them with arms around each other's shoulders. The important point is, "Let them be." Do not pressure for your gain. Do not become enraged because your child happens to be enraged at that hour. Do allow your child a reasonably free rein in choosing his frends (or enemies). Do not try to apply the standards of the adult to assess the value of a particular friendship among children. The "old man" may be a thief, but his child might just suit your child's needs at that hour or day or month.

Some exceptionally bright children may seek out friends who are older because of common intellectual interests. Others may seek out friends who are younger because they may feel threatened for some reason by children their age. Trying to understand such needs may help towards alleviating the pressures on such a child. In the great majority of cases, a hands-off policy is best. When should we intervene? A case in point is the "villainous hero."

The Villainous Hero

In a threatening world, the child seeks to protect himself with a mantle of power. Where is such power obtained? Partially from people who appear to the child to have power and strength. Children will therefore identify with the aggressor because the aggressor seems to have the power. It is as though by standing close to the aggressor and taking on his characteristics the frightened child will also be covered by the aggressor's umbrella of strength. The aggression may be a manifestation of fear, but to the admiring child this will not be obvious. All that he feels is that emulating the aggressor makes him relatively safe.

Usually the "Villainous hero" is somewhat older than the other children, and usually the product of a broken home or an unhealthy relationships between parents. Antisocial acts are such a child's reaction to the threatening world. Stealing and truancy are common among the younger ones, and use of drugs, gambling, and sexual promiscuity are the vices of the older ones. To some children they become heroes—because they seem to have power—no matter what villains they are to the adult. When such a situation arises, it becomes necessary to trip the villainous hero's façade of power away and expose the naked frightened child beneath. Parents who become wise in the ways of children can do this without having to wait for the truant officer or the policeman.

Parties and Not Poopers

The opportunity for parents to set aside a special day for each child presents itself once a year on the child's birthday. Having a birthday party can be very good for the child, but it can also cause chaos, tears, and distraught parents.

Last year my eldest son's best friend sat in a tree crying while below his mother tried to conduct a birthday party for his younger brother.

To prevent tears and retreat to the trees, let's see what we can do and what we should not do.

For Whom the Billowing Balloons?

A child's birthday should be his day, if possible. It should not be a day for mother to fulfill her social obligations to friends and relatives. It is a day for the child to receive individual attention, love, and, of course, gifts.

Whom to invite can at times be a ticklish situation, for your child may detest your best friend's child. Within reason the guests and part of the arrangements, depending of course on the age, should be in accord with your child's wishes. Remember, it's his day and not yours.

You might be tempted by the thought of substituting a special gift for a noisy, hectic party. This might be a satisfactory agreement, providing that this is the child's preference, not the mother's. Often, long after the toy has lost its appeal, a child decides he somehow missed out on something other children have.

Out of the Trees and Helping

Handling brotherly hate can sometimes pose a problem at a birthday party. If the older brothers and sisters can be employed as assistants, it can alleviate two problems. It will help diminish the jealousy felt when the other is getting all of the attention, and also younger children usually admire an older child and will more readily participate in activities directed by him. With this in mind, we hired our nine-year-old son and his friend to set up and run a carnival for our five-year-old daughter. It proved quite successful for everyone.

Preventing Chaos

Children's behavior will vary greatly at any party—depending on their age, the stimulation they are subjected to and, of course, each individual personality.

AT ONE:

Attempting any celebration with one-year-olds is inviting disaster. Children this age are incapable of comprehending the situation and find the wrappings more fascinating than the presents or their guests. Overwhelmed and confused by the commotion, the gala social affair usually ends with several tots in tears. This day, however, holds a great deal of sentimental significance for you as parents, and a small, quiet family celebration would prove satisfying.

AT TWO:

A small birthday cake and candles, a familiar playmate and a feeling of warmth and love create a party for the two-year-old.

AT THREE:

Most three-year-olds have matured to the point where they happily anticipate a party. A short, simple function with a few friends is most feasible. You will find it easier to allow the children to play by themselves in an informal setting rather than attempting group activity. It is difficult for children to follow directions at this age. Supplying them with crayons,

paper and toys provides a pleasant afternoon. If there are
some toys about which your child is very possessive it might
be wise to get them out of sight. It is unreasonable to expect a
three-year-old to gladly share all his treasures, and avoiding a
conflict is better than arguing it out.

Children this age are not usually socially secure enough to
attend a party without mother there. Some might spend days
eagerly asking how much longer it will be before the party
starts and then cling tearfully to mother throughout the party.
Others start quarrels over some small object. This is one time
when it is preferable to "treat the symptom, not the disease."
Don't try to understand why Donald is spilling soda on
Karen—just get him to stop as quickly as possible.

FROM FOUR TO SIX:

Celebrations for children from four to six are at best
exciting, hectic, and exhausting for parents and children. I
would suggest facing the day armed with a sensibly prepared
plan, small prizes for each guest, simple refreshments, a
grin-and-bear-it attitude, and possibly some aspirin nearby. I
cannot overemphasize pre-planning, as idle little hands get
into mischief, each other's toys, and your breakable treasures.

Although children between four and six eagerly anticipate
a party, there are several kinds of party poopers who can turn
a happy occasion into a bedlam. Joe, the hyperactive, ram-
bunctious child, can incite all the guests to silly, wild behavior; Steven, the aggressive one, can decide someone ate his
candy and punch the nearest child; Alice is in tears because
she is "allergic" to the food or doesn't want to eat the cake;
Robert won't let mother out of his sight; Barbara, the non-
joiner, won't become part of any game. Where does one
begin? Again, try treating each upheaval as quickly and
simply as possible. Try getting Joe involved in helping with
the party, giving out toys, leading games; give Steven extra
candy; tell Alice she need not eat anything if she doesn't want
to.

FROM SEVEN TO NINE:

Between the ages of seven and nine children begin to show
a degree of sophistication at birthday parties. They more

readily show the individuality one might expect at an adult cocktail party. There is the shy guest, the one who has difficulty becoming part of a group; the over-boisterous one who demands the spotlight; the spoiler, who insists the ice cream is sour and Joe's (or his) party was better.

It is only a party and not group therapy, so merely direct your efforts to keeping the children as busy as possible in organized play.

At this age children (in small numbers) readily take to a small number of them being taken to some amusement center for games, hot dogs, and hamburgers. Such sports as bowling, skating, or seeing a baseball game are often better appreciated than the usual games at home.

AT TEN:

At ten many children have no desire for the usual party. They have matured to a point where some may want to have just one or two good friends and their own immediate family for dinner at home or in a restaurant. Girls at ten and a little younger like to have pajama sleep-in parties on a weekend night.

Within reason a parent can acquiesce to the standards of his community in what kind of party he has for his child. Of course, the amount of money spent should be determined by his needs, not his child's or neighbors' or relatives'.

Safaris Not Necessary

There is the story about the man who wanted a confirmation party for his son that would be most unique and impressive. After much consultation with experts in the field of gala social events, he eagerly agreed to have a safari into the jungles of Africa. Who but the wisest and wealthiest could have thought of such a party? And so there they were, all the relatives riding atop elephants to a jungle clearing for the most unique confirmation yet held. Suddenly the chief guide held up his hand and called a halt to the procession. The worried father asked what was wrong. The guide answered,

"We can't move ahead till the safari in front leaves the clearing. They're holding a confirmation party."

Parents can rightfully feel proud of raising their children and showing their love and devotion. But is it necessary to spend large sums of money for gaudy affairs? Too often it is a parent's need to increase his own status that has him insist that "only the biggest and the best will do," whether the child is having a tenth, or thirteenth, or sweet-sixteenth birthday party—or a wedding reception.

I have seen situations where children actually cried to have small, simple affairs only to have one of the parents insist on "only the best."

A child who has been exposed to proper values will readily adhere to any small budget set aside for his party. If it is the child who insists on the "biggest and best," it is the parental influence that ought to be looked into, and rarely just the influence of his peers.

Present Perfect

A brief word on gifts. Often a child is in a better position to know what his friends want than we are. We may be tempted to buy an article of clothing only to have the recipient exclaim, "My mother buys me clothes anyway. That's not a present." Our children need acceptance by their peers as well as from us. If the child feels a particular game is what he would like to bring as a gift and it is within the price range you want to spend, that becomes the present perfect.

Here, again, is an opportunity for our children to learn values. The parent whose need is to stand out and have status may attempt to have his child bring the largest and most expensive gift. Doing so could well have your child feeling uncomfortable in later years at social functions, particularly when he has to pay the bills for gifts or contributions.

Teacher Troubles and
Troubled Teachers

Since each child is unique it would follow that each adult is unique. Some adults become teachers. They have varied feelings and varied backgrounds as do most any other adults. Some are kindly and understanding of children and some are not. Some are better adjusted than others. Just as parents, they have their preferences and prejudices. They have their good days and bad days. They are human, just as we are.

As teachers they play a most important role in the lives of our children and hence in our lives as well. Many of our children glide through school, others have difficulties. Often I have heard parents exclaim, "The teacher doesn't like him," as the reason for his school difficulties. Some parents are quick to blame the teacher for their children's difficulties and some parents are fearful and do nothing when their child is being harmed by the teacher. I feel it is important that we get some clarification and better understanding of our role as parents when our child is having "Teacher Troubles."

The Teacher as the Expert

Some teachers have a good grasp of child development and are warm people. Others are quite ignorant of what a child is like at a given age and are cold fish. Some I have found to be cruel and vindictive. It is therefore wrong to accept every teacher's word as the gospel truth.

Here, again, it is essential that we know our child and can be objective regarding any comments a teacher may have about him. We should know our child's strengths and weaknesses. Seeing things objectively and accepting our child will help us make a true evaluation of our child's academic and social progress. It lets the parent side with the teacher when necessary and to side with the child when the teacher is wrong. As parents, when we make an error, we ought to be able to admit it to our children. There should never be the attitude of "Right or wrong, the parent is right." Nor should there be an attitude of "Right or wrong, the teacher is right." Each situation must be judged on its own merits.

When your child tells you of an episode in which he feels the teacher acted wrongly and this is verified by others and you feel convinced that your child is correct, it is in your child's best interest to side with him. *Do be certain* that you have all the facts. In the past the attitude that a teacher or other authority figure could do no wrong prevailed. To continue this approach is to have your child feel righteously aggrieved and abandoned when he needs you most.

Moon Money

Let us realize that as parents and taxpayers it is we who largely determine the caliber of teaching in our schools. Next to us, teachers perform the most important function in helping our children adjust to the complicated world outside. Teaching a class of children is no easy matter. It is a good feeling to know a teacher will take the time necessary to understand our child and help him along the way. But such help cannot be given when there are large numbers of children in each class. Paying low salaries, thereby losing better qualified people, cheats our children, too.

If we can spend billions of dollars trying to get one man to the moon, surely we have the funds to get our children educated so that they can stand solidly on earth.

Death Deals a Blow

To the living, the finality of death is incomprehensible. Man's mind cannot conceive of a state of nothingness—death. Through the ages man has had fantasies of some form of life in the hereafter. When an Egyptian Pharaoh died, his servants, supplies, provisions, and a vessel for travel to the "hereafter" were entombed with him. The concept of reincarnation has within it the belief in a form of perpetual existence.

Since the adult with his greater experience and learning finds it so difficult to tolerate the idea of death, how do we help our children when such a problem arises?

No Comfort in Our Comfort

If we are to be in a position to help our children with the trauma of the death of someone close, then we must realize that a young child does not perceive death as we do. What may comfort us may not comfort him. We may, if we are Catholics, derive comfort from the thought of heaven. But to the child, all he knows is that someone who had much meaning for him is gone—the concept of heaven holds no comfort for him.

As in matters of sex, what can be said to a child regarding death will vary with the particular circumstances in each family. Certainly the death of a pet, however close and loving, will not have the same traumatizing effect as the death of a close realtive, be it sibling, parent, or grandparent. The age of the child and his ability to tolerate stress are all factors to be considered.

It is not possible to list here the many times when the question of death might arise, but I feel that we should have some understanding of how a child's mind perceives death at a given age. The greater our understanding of a child's feelings about death, the better we will be able to help the child if such help becomes necessary.

How Long Is Forever?

"Will Laddie be dead for the rest of his life?" "Yes." "Forever and forever and forever?" These were the questions asked by my five-year-old daughter, Sharon, when our neighbors' dog was killed several months ago. It well illustrates that a five-year-old has not developed the concept of time as we know it. The question has within it the idea of reversibility of death—as though after some time Laddie will again be as he had been.

The usual ease with which a calm five-year-old accepts death changes during the next four years. At about the age of nine or ten children have a fairly good grasp of the irreversibility of death, know that death may come from various causes and that they and their loved ones must eventually die. Between the ages of six and eight we see varied responses regarding death. Some children who find a dead bird,—or, in the case of my children, when their toad died—make elaborate burial arrangements. As each child is unique, what we say and how we say it should be tempered by our evaluation of a child's sensitivity. What we expect of a child in the face of the death of someone close should, of course, take into consideration the child's needs. This does not mean we lie to the child or evade his questions. It does require that we see the child as a child, we cannot expect from him what we might from an adult.

What about having children at burial services? I do not think it wise to have a child who is younger than ten view the actual lowering of the casket. Better to have children help with chores about the home at such times. The lowering of someone close into the earth and the hysteria of some adults may well be too traumatizing for the most stable youngster.

You and I

Should a very close relative such as a parent or sibling die, a child will show what I have called the *I* of the ch*I*ld. I think it is important that I repeat this essential self-concept of the child. To a child's way of thinking and feeling, everything revolves around him. When a parent or a sibling or even a pet dies, a young child is certain to ask what role he played in the death. This is well illustrated by the question of an eight-year-old girl whose father died at an early age. "Do you think he died because I didn't kiss him good-night? I really wasn't angry." The child seems to feel that she *did* something, that her anger contributed to his death.

When a parent dies, a child may openly express the feeling that the surviving parent should have done more to prevent the other parent's death. Not only does the child feel that he is so omnipotent that his anger can kill, he feels his parent is omnipotent and has the power of life and death. He may therefore feel that you are in some way responsible for the very death you mourn. It sometimes becomes necessary to repeat and repeat and reassure and reassure—letting him know again and again that *he* is not responsible.

On Suicide

Should a suicide occur in a family, its traumatic impact will shake the healthiest of people and will be most disturbing to young children. Here again, the child will think of the many normal things that happened between himself and the deceased and wonder about his role in the suicide. Adults may do this as well, but a child's mind sees only itself and knows nothing of the true circumstances that may have led to someone's suicide.

It is difficult enough to tell a child that someone has died. How much more difficult it is for someone to tell the child that the death was self-inflicted. Physical illness and resulting death can be understood far better than mental illness and self-destruction.

With 22,000 recorded suicides a year in the United States

and probably just as many more recorded as "accidental," the difficult task of informing a child of a parent's or sibling's suicide faces many of us. Do we hide the truth? What do we say? Each situation is unique, so no one answer will suffice. I would therefore suggest to any parent who faces such an awful dilemma that the following be considered:

Help Needed

Should a child have an infection, we take him to a pediatrician or family doctor for antibotics. We also see to it that our child gets "shots" to prevent such infectious diseases as smallpox. But what do we do to prevent any mental illness when a child is exposed to a far more traumatizing situation than a bacillus infection? Usually very little. We don't play doctor with possible physical illness. There are times when a physician trained in the care of the mental illnesses of children should also be consulted. This is particularly true when there has been a suicide in the family. A child psychiatrist can offer the needed guidance to the surviving parent (or parents, if it is a brother or sister who committed suicide).

The guilt, the anger, the gnawing doubts of a child are much too much for any parent to deal with, no matter how wise and intelligent he may be. This is not a matter he can easily cope with unless there is some professional help.

Shall I Tell?

Childhood is difficult enough. The adopted child not only faces the difficulty of growing up, he also has to endure the pains of doubt—the doubt that gnaws at him regarding why he was "given away." Here, again, the *I* of the child's mind plays an important role. The young child cannot conceive of ill parents or the death of parents without feeling that somehow "I" had something to do with it. So the adopted child often feels, "I must have been bad"—or in some way responsible for his being given up for adoption.

Some parents, for fear of what it might do to the child, or from their own need for people to think the child was naturally theirs, hesitate to tell the adopted child the truth. It is a dangerous game. Too many children have been shocked and hurt when they learned the truth by accident or through the malice of some adult or child. The answer to the question "Shall I tell?" is an unqualified "Yes."

When and How

Some agencies recommend to the adoptive parents that their child be told of his adoption as early as possible. At a clinic one day I was astonished to hear a mother singing a song to her newly adopted three-month-old infant about his having been adopted. Sounds ridiculous, doesn't it? I think so.

The time to begin is with small doses when they are just about beginning to have an awareness of birth and might ask where they came from. Here, again, the situation will vary in each family. The sight of a pregnant relative or pet may have your adopted child ask you if you also had an enlarged stomach and carried him in similar fashion. As with questions on sex, a complete and unabridged answer all at once is not necessary. You can merely state that all children are born in a similar fashion. Varying with the circumstances in each family, telling the child that he was chosen in a very wonderful and special way should be accomplished by the age of about seven or eight. Of course, the task is much easier when the parents really feel that way about the adoption. Where there is anger and guilt about not having a natural child, the task becomes quite difficult for the parents. But it must be done, and by the parents—not by a third party.

Parents who feel good about the adoption will impart such a feeling to the child. By the time a child is seven or eight he can feel, along with his parents, joy in having a complete family. He can be given to understand that in his parents the reproductive mechanism was faulty and they therefore went to a special agency to choose the child they wanted.

A Picture Plan

A child of seven cannot recall events such as birthdays at the age of one and two. He certainly can't remember your joy in taking him home from the hospital or adoption agency. To parents who are going to adopt a child I should like to suggest some simple procedures that may add a little more to the adopted child's feeling that he was really wanted by you. Simply take pictures (still or movie) of your picking him up at the agency or hospital. If there is a time lapse between his birth date and adoption date, what is wrong in having two dates to celebrate? Have pictures taken of these celebrations each year. All this will let the adopted child really feel the acceptance you try to convey. You can go a long way through these means to counter his doubts about why he was given away.

A Continuous Need

In the chapter "Brotherly Hate," I spoke of continually reassuring each child of your love. The adopted child requires such reassurance a little more. Sometimes a lot more, as I will describe below.

No child's life is free of difficulties which you will find it necessary to criticize. At such times an adopted child might cry out, "You're not my real father!" or "You're not my real mother!" Such an outburst is the child's way of seeking assurance that your criticism will not change your wanting him as your child. At such a time, the simple answer is, "Of course I'm your father." (Or, "Of course I'm your mother.")

Double Jeopardy

Because of progress recently made in the area of fertility drugs, more couples who adopted a child during barren years have gone on to having their own natural child. A time of great rejoicing for the parents becomes a time of double jeopardy for the older adopted child. Not only does he have a rival, that rival has come directly from the mother's body. It will make the adopted child feel that he could never approach the closeness that his rival has and will continue to have with his mother. It is therefore necessary that parents be aware of the double jeopardy their older child feels. He will look to see if there is any truth in his fears. At such times parents will find themselves hard pressed to prove to the adopted child that their love for him has not diminished. There is the temptation to yield a little more to the adopted child's demands. Then the parents are really on a tightrope because the child will ask if they yield because in fact they feel guilty about their feelings towards him. Treating the adopted child and the natural child as full equals is therefore the best approach.

Choose with Care

Having a child and raising a child should always be a joint venture. It is not wise for the childless woman to force her husband against his wishes to adopt a child, nor a childless man to force his reluctant wife. A woman may do so in an attempt to fulfill strong mothering urges within her, or she may feel the need of a child to save her marriage. Whatever the reason, it is essential that there be two fully accepting adoptive parents.

Once a positive decision is made, the wisest move is to seek out a reputable agency or organization that will help you to find the child you seek. It is foolish and dangerous to adopt a child who has not been properly evaluated both physically and mentally. Reputable agencies will see to it that only a healthy child is placed with adoptive parents.

He Won't Be Living
Here Any More

Divorce is the most obvious situation in which the needs of the parents come into direct conflict with the basic needs of the child. With more than one out of every four marriages ending in divorce, many among parents with young children, we can appreciate the seriousness of a problem that tears at the very heart of both parent and child.

To those parents who face such a difficult situation, I should like to mention some factors they may not clearly understand. Perhaps with understanding, a difficult situation may be easier to live with for parent and child.

Who's to Blame?

Questions that are sure to come to a marriage partner with marital difficulties are: Whose fault is it? Am I to blame? If only I . . . would this have occurred? Where did I fail?

The answer is that it is quite possible that neither parent is at fault or has failed in any way. Allow me to explain. Each of us is molded by forces over which we have no control. As adults we are the products of our childhoods, products of events. How we act or think in later years is the product of those early years when things were done *to* us, when we had no control over events. In my discussion of "Children in Parents' Clothing" I mentioned a few of the factors which may influence an adult to behave in a manner incompatible with the responsibilities of parenthood—or the responsibilities of marriage.

We cannot see or understand the forces that molded us. If we are to gain understanding of people, we must for the moment set aside such terms as "blame" and "fault" and the morality of any situation.

Infidelity

A common reason for divorce is infidelity. We need not condone it. Some alleged experts in the field of human relations go so far as to recommend extramarital affairs. Such ideas are ridiculous. I know of no responsible psychiatrist who recommends it. But it does require understanding by those whose lives have been shattered by it.

Mr. and Mrs. R., like many another couple, had their home broken up by infidelity. Mrs. R. was raised by an inadequate mother and an alcoholic father. In later years, she could recall being fearful of her father's wrath, yet wanting very much to be close to him. Her relationships with men had a similar pattern. In her teen years her desire to gain a feeling of closeness with the opposite sex led her into promiscuity. Although she frequently had sex, she gained no gratification. When she was eighteen and met Mr. R., she truly felt she was in love. He was twenty-five, good-looking, had a fine job, treated her well—all the things she felt she wanted so much. Within the year they married, and little Robert was born soon after.

But Mrs. R. still felt unfulfilled. During sexual intercourse she went through "an act," as she phrased it. She had her husband believing that she thoroughly enjoyed it, but all the while she wondered what it was like to be a "Lady Chatterley." Within two years, little Dennis was born. Saddled with two small sons, with Mr. R. working long hours toward a better position, feeling unfulfilled sexually, Mrs. R. began to feel angry and discontent. One summer, while vacationing with the children at a resort while Mr. R. labored in the city, she had her first extramarital affair with a member of the hotel staff. Any satisfaction? No. Still there lingered unfulfilled desires. That year there were several more affairs, seldom twice with the same man.

Mr. R. finally became aware of what was happening when a neighbor's wife called. When he confronted her, Mrs. R. felt quite guilty—she admitted to having the affair with the neighbor and added a little more. It was too much for Mr. R. A shocked, nauseous feeling overcame him. He left the house that night and never returned. After the anger came the doubts. Where did he fail? If only he could have satisfied her!

The simple truth is that no man could have done what Mr. R. wished he could do. Long after the divorce he felt inadequate, ashamed of his choice of a mate, fearful that marriage would again bring similar difficulties.

Both Mr. and Mrs. R. eventually sought psychiatric help; Mrs. R. to gain insight into the needs that still left her unfulfilled, and Mr. R. to learn that there are times when there can be problems in others that do not necessarily reflect shortcomings in oneself.

In similar fashion, the woman who discovers her husband has been unfaithful or whose husband leaves her for another woman usually becomes depressed. She sees herself as somehow failing to satisfy him, as not having the qualities he seeks. In most of these cases the man himself doesn't know what he is seeking. Rarely is the wife able to realize that it might be her husband's problems that drive him to other conquests.

It would help considerably if the injured parties were able to see that what may have gone wrong in their marriage was a difficulty in which they played a small role—the major part having been played years before when the "wrongdoer" was a child.

When parents are able to see the true situation with objectivity, the difficult task of being a divorced parent becomes somewhat easier. There can be a failure in marriage; there need not be a failure in parenthood.

Do Not Destroy

A parent in the midst of a divorce and after a divorce will normally run the gamut of emotions. There may be intense hate where love formerly existed. There may be valid reasons for the hate, but it is important that it not lead to an attempt to destroy one's former mate. Such destruction can lead to the destruction of the healthy self-image any child desperately needs.

The following sounds melodramatic, I admit, but it does put into a few words a truth about child development. Hate your mate but do not destroy—for the individual you destroy may be your child.

A mother who feels wronged could very well ask, "Are you trying to have me tell my child that the horror I was married to is really a saint?" No, I am not. But continue telling your child what a horrible man he is and your son will be sure to feel something horrible about himself. A daughter may begin to have the feeling that all men are horrors and should be shunned. In a similar fashion, the father who openly berates his former wife in front of their children will leave a daughter feeling uncomfortable about herself and a son questioning the goodness of any girl or woman.

An Essential for Mental Health

A bad marriage partner can still be a good parent.

A child is healthiest when he can build from those around him. The material that he uses to build his image of himself is the material he sees and feels around him. If he is told that the quality of the material around him is worthless, he will in all likelihood feel worthless as well. That is why it is so necessary that parents be able to separate in their own minds those qualities in their mates which led to marital difficulties from those qualities which can have value in the lives of their children.

Who's on Whose Side?

Your need during a divorce may be to have everyone agree with you, including your children. You may want them to side with you. But a child needs two parents; he is concerned with his needs, not yours.

He needs to continue to have two parents, to be loved and cared for by both of them. It is unfair and unwise for him to be subjected to a power-play between two opposing giants, for he is fearful of incurring the wrath of either.

A Little Goes a Long Way

The parent who relinquishes custody of his child will wonder how he can possibly continue to have a healthy influence on his child's emotional development when he spends so little time with him. The answer is that a little is far better than none, and that a little time goes a long way. Even a phone call, a letter, a brief greeting, are a child's stepping stones for further growth. Children are quite astute at knowing who really loves and cares for them. A ten-cent phone call or picture-postcard can mean more than the most expensive plaything.

It's You and *I* Again

As with illness and death, the *I* of the child's mind plays a big role in how he perceives a divorce between his parents.

The little girl who loves her daddy so much will wonder whether her love for him was the factor that led to her parents' parting. The little boy who sees his father as a rival (all little boys do) will come away feeling that his wish has come true. He will now have his mother all for himself and he will feel threatened by his father's wrath.

We are again dealing with a child's mind, which always sees itself directly involved in all the things which go on around him.

The divorced parent need not be shocked when a child blames him for the loss of his other parent. We are dealing here with a child's perception of his parent as so powerful that if the parent chose to he could cure the marriage and prevent a divorce.

When the *I* comes up in conversation, and it certainly will at least be thought about, the parent should patiently listen and try in simple, honest language to explain how the divorce did not occur because of anything the child has done.

When the matter of *you* is brought up, again explain in simple language that there can be goodness in people and yet differences which pervent a happy marriage.

Do not expect a child to come away convinced of what you say. It will take time and repetition for the truth to make sense to a young mind.

When a Doctor Is Needed

Normally a child's life is filled with stresses and strains, ups and downs. How do we tell when a situation warrants talking things over with a doctor? In mental health as in physical health there are questions we can ask about a particular symptom. When did it begin? How long has it lasted? How severe or incapacitating is it? What other signs or symptoms are associated with the main difficulty?

When Did It Begin?

The age of a patient and his circumstances are most important in evaluating a symptom. If a boy of fifteen complained of chest pains after eating a whole pizza pie we would not be as concerned as we would be for the fifty-year-old man complaining of the same pain after shoveling snow off his walk. Similarly, a child of five who is bed-wetting will not cause us as much concern as a child of ten, or a child who had been trained and then begins to wet the bed. The child who shows anger towards his mother after the birth of a sibling is quite different from the child who shows continual anger without any known cause.

How Long Has It Lasted!

We wouldn't consult our doctor if we coughed for a day, but we would be foolish to go on coughing daily for a month without paying attention to it. Similarly, we wouldn't pay much attention to a child feeling sad and wanting to be alone for a day. We certainly should find ourselves concerned if it lasted for weeks.

How Severe Is It?

The child who requests that a light remain on in his room need not trouble us, but the child who so fears the dark that he insists a parent be in bed with him and panics on awakening when he is alone has a problem which is far more severe and warrants obtaining help.

What Else?

A simple symptom is certainly not as much a danger sign as multiple symptoms. The child who taunts his younger brother may be looked upon as showing simple "brotherly hate." But if he shows aggression towards other children, is a bed-wetter, an underachiever at school, and takes delight in torturing animals, then we have to agree that a problem exists that needs professional help.

Problems That Need Looking Into

The following are listed in a roughly chronological order, with the earliest difficulties listed first.

Some of these signs and symptoms can be seen easily and will probably be observed by both you and your pediatrician or family doctor.

1—Shows lack of interest in children and people around him.

2—Refuses to participate in B.M. toilet training after the second year.

3—Lacks some normal speech after the second year.

4—Marked hyperactivity, often associated with poor coordination and delayed speech.

5—Marked destructiveness.

6—Refuses after age of four to part from mother, despite all efforts.

7—Continual aggression towards other children.

8—Multiple fears of normal living, such as being hurt by other children, darkness, animals, being alone.

9—Daily bed-wetting after age five.

10—Fear of going to school; gives all kinds of excuses, such as stomach aches and headaches, on the mornings of school days.

11—Chronic uninterest in life around him.

12—Fire-setting.

13—Chronic school difficulties, such an underachieving and truancy.

14—Refusal to separate from family, such as going to sleep-away camp after age ten.

15—Chronic excessive playing with genitals.

16—Chronic lying and cheating, particularly after age of ten.

17—Inability to make friends.

Seeking Qualified Help

When parents feel a problem exists, whom are they to see? With whom do they consult? When it comes to emotional difficulties, parents are often faced with decisions that they cannot make because they do not have the knowledge.

The field of mental health is today where physiological medicine was at the turn of the century, before Flexner pointed out the vast differences that existed in the training of physicians. Today there are rigid standards for all medical colleges and students.

Sadly, there are no such standards in the field of mental health. Anyone can call himself a therapist. There are probably more people being seen in so-called treatment by alleged therapists than are being seen by qualified personnel.

I remember one day when a neighbor asked me why I had had to spend so many years in psychiatric training. She knew of another neighbor, a school teacher, who was spending two evenings a week in training and after two years at his "institute" he was going to be "qualified" as a "child therapist." I also began to wonder about this sad state of affairs when one day that same school teacher asked to borrow my Grey's text on anatomy. He was going to study it for that week and learn neuroanatomy. Neuroanatomy in several hours? It takes almost that long just to turn all the pages.

The need for people in the field of mental health is so great that it pays for many to do "therapy," qualified or not. In many institutions and clincs a team approach is employed. There is a physician, trained in psychiatry, the psychologist, and the social worker. That is fine. It is when poorly trained personnel attempt to separate the mind from the brain and the rest of the body that difficulties arise.

A case in point was four-year-old David, whom I saw. He could not talk, was markedly hyperactive, and at times would find himself preoccupied with building blocks. His mother had become pregnant with David only three months after having given birth to a daughter. She never wanted David and felt quite guilty. She found herself overburdened with two young infants. When David was thirty months old, she sought help for his hyperactivity and muteness. She was told that David was autistic and that she required therapy because of her hostility and anger toward him. David's mother felt even more guilty and entered into twice-a-week therapy. After a year of talking about her guilt, David was as ill as ever.

There was a major difficulty in all of this. The non-medical individual who was seeing her privately and made the diagnosis had overlooked an important factor—David was organically brain-damaged, that is, he had, during birth or possibly before, sustained damage to his brain so that it could not function properly. True, his mother's attitude did not help matters. But she could have sat and discussed her guilt for twenty years and David would have remained the same or gotten worse. What was missed was that David was born after a very difficult and prolonged labor and was cyanotic at birth. David's brain never really developed normally—and not just because of his mother. The mind can do just about everything (as in hysterical paralysis), but it doesn't produce brain damage.

This is not told to disparage the non-medical personnel in the field of mental health. They are urgently needed. It does show the limitations in the training of non-medical people. It is essential that diagnosis be made by medical people who have been trained to see every aspect of a man's functions.

When David was put on medication, he became much less hyperactive and became cooperative enough to be accepted for special schooling.

In other situations, I and other psychiatrists find ourselves frustrated and angry when we are brought in to see a depressed or agitated child or adult who has been going downhill while under the care of some poorly trained lay person in private practice. The simple use of new medication would, in many situations, have made a difference between functioning at home and hospitalization. Since only physicians such as psychiatrists can prescribe medication, the advent of many new drugs which can help enormously in mental illness makes a team approach essential. The difficulty is that sometimes everyone wants to be "the surgeon." Can you imagine the chaos in an operating room with everyone there trying to operate? That is the problem we face in mental health.

It is a problem that need not face the parent of a child who shows signs and symptoms of having emotional difficulties. *First* discuss them with your pediatrician or family doctor. He is in a far better position to know what is normal or abnormal for your child than the individual whose name you might find in the yellow pages under "counseling" or "hypnosis" or a score of other non-medical headings.

Even school difficulties should be discussed with your doctor. An underachiever, for example, can have any number of problems such as poor vision or hearing or perceptual difficulties that will hinder his ability to learn.

Your pediatrician or your family doctor may suggest a diagnosis by a child psychiatrist. Or he may refer you to a child psychologist, or perhaps he feels the family needs the help of a psychiatric social worker. Many people are confused by the difference between psychiatrist and psychologist. The child psychiatrist is a physician who has specialized in psychiatry in a three-year program and then has studied child psychiatry for at least two years. He spends as many years in training as does a surgeon.

The psychologist is not a physician, but has been trained at a graduate school and has obtained a doctorate (Ph.D.) in the field of psychology. He has been trained to give and interpret the findings of psychological tests. In addition, many have received further training and experience in treating some forms of mental illness. The psychiatric social worker has been trained not only in social work, but has received further training and experience in dealing with emotionally ill people and their families.

The Ostriches

We have become more sophisticated in the language of psychiatry. Parents at a cocktail party can talk glibly of Freud and Jung, but if one of their children shows some indication of disturbance, all too frequently they behave like ostriches.

One of the most difficult and frustrating problems for anyone involved in the emotional development of children is to be confronted by parents who behave like ostriches. These are parents who are afraid to see a part of themselves which they would rather reject or have repressed. They feel so guilty that when their children show some difficulty they immediately take it as a reflection upon themselves.

It is estimated that approximately fifty per cent of children with emotional difficulties cannot be effectively helped because their parents are too fearful of becoming involved. Guidance counselors at schools tell me they have to send telegrams to parents who cut off phone service or have numbers unlisted. Letters go unanswered by parents who try to prevent school officials from reaching them.

For parents who feel so threatened, I should like to make several points.

1—Many of the problems children have are the normal pains of development and you are often not responsible.

2—The goal of anyone whose task is to help your child is to help you as well. They are well aware of the difficulties of raising any child. I am referring to the teachers, counselors, school psychologists, and psychiatrists whose job is to make life easier for both child and parent.

3—Do not be fearful that your "impurities" will be detected or have to be fully discussed before your child can be helped. At times full discussion is required, but it is to help both parent and child, never to condemn the parent.

Once I was consulted about a teen-age girl who was truant and had more than the average school difficulties. In our first interview, her mother felt the need to confess an "indiscretion" of years before. I have no doubt that mother's guilt plagued her so that neither mother nor daughter ever followed through on getting help. A phone call canceling our next interview removed the chance of helping mother or daughter. The mother chose the ostrich role, one that offers only very temporary refuge.

Preventing Future Difficulties

Child psychiatry is in its infancy in the prevention of mental illness. The pediatrician has a full armamentarium to prevent physical illness. If only we had the equivalent for mental illness! We don't, but there are some situations that bring with them so much mental anguish that I feel we ought to discuss them. I am referring to such situations as death and divorce or other traumatic situations. We don't hesitate to have a child take painful anti-rabies vaccine if he is bitten. But too often we drag our feet when it comes to preventing future mental distress. We need not and should not.

A Last Note

If the briefest summary of a parent's role in the healthy mental development of a child could be simply stated the following would be listed:

To accept, love, and protect—but not to smother.

To assist but not to push.

To understand how a child's mind operates and what his needs are and thus to communicate better.

To set an example for the world's greatest mimics, our children.

To have as our goal his ultimate happiness, based truly on his needs and not on ours.

If these pages have brought some understanding, perhaps some comfort, to parents, then I shall consider my efforts worthwhile.

It is impossible in any text to answer the myriad questions that arise in the rearing of a particular child. I would welcome any comments or questions parents may have about the emotional development of their children. Merely address your inquiry to me care of my publisher, Pocket Books, 630 Fifth Avenue, New York, N.Y. 10020.

I shall do my utmost to answer those questions which can be handled by correspondence.

Index

Today they're playing word games.
Before he's five, he can be reading 150 words a minute.

HOW TO GIVE YOUR CHILD A SUPERIOR MIND

A remarkable new book tells how you, yourself—at home—with no special training can actually add as much as thirty points to your child's effective I.Q....how you can help him move ahead quickly in school and enable him to be more successful in an education-conscious world.

Best of all, your child can achieve this early success without being pushed and without interference with a happy, normal, well-adjusted childhood.

GIVE YOUR CHILD A SUPERIOR MIND provides a planned program of home instruction that any parent can start using immediately. *You will learn:*

1. How to awaken your child's inborn desire to learn.
2. How to teach your child to read.
3. How to help your child streak ahead in math.
4. How to give your child the power of abstract reasoning.
5. How to increase your child's effective I.Q.

At all bookstores, or mail coupon today.

75395